Preface

Nature Notes is a personal nature diary which is published each Saturday in the 'Cumberland and Westmorland Herald' of Penrith, Cumbria. This, the first collection, gathers together the first year and a half of the Notes and takes us from the height of summer activity in August 1995 to the snowy end of 1996.

The aim of the Notes is to share with readers the treasures to be found all around us; the pleasure, surprises and fun that I find while looking at and wondering about our landscape and its inhabitants.

There's no need to trek out to nature reserves to experience wild life. Nature creeps and walks and flies into the town and village. Old walls, churchyards, hedges, roadside trees and verges, and gardens are crammed with things to identify and to investigate. Practically everything in the diaries has been observed in easily- accessible public places or from the windows of car or home. But of course Cumbria does have exceptionally wild spots both high on the fells and wellie-deep in the bogs. Some special creatures live there and from time to time these make an appearance.

If any reader is inspired to pause at a pond in summer and spot a dragonfly emerging to adult beauty fr[illegible]'s fiendish underwater nymph, the wings exp[illegible] rumpled silk to sheer gauze, or in a [illegible]ecreeper walking up th[illegible]stion like why do clo[illegible]lions close at night, th[illegible]orthwhile.

Frances B[illegible]

Penrith.
October 1997

ISBN 1.900821.22.2

Published by

RegentLane Ltd
Devonshire Road Industrial Estate
Millom, Cumbria LA18 4JS

Cover illustration by Marianne Birkby

Photographs and Pencil sketches by the author.

5th August

If I were asked to name a place where elves might come to dance, it would have to be the woodland glade where I'm keeping cool on an otherwise roastingly-hot hillside. Outside, on the screes, the stones are too hot to touch and the bilberries are also hot - a strange experience to eat hot fruit straight off the plant. But in this wood where ancient oaks spread smooth silver-white branches over a soft and green mossy lawn, it's totally different. It's a secret, fairytale place. Sunlight dapples trees and waving grass, chaffinches and tits play above in the leafy branches. The backdrop through the trees is the green mountain flank of Aikin Knott.

This wood, though not of course individual trees, may well be a survivor of the original forest which covered the fells in prehistoric times. Around Derwentwater this contained oak and would have been managed so as to make the most of this timber tree. If so, this hillside has always been wooded, and the wood lived through the millennia that saw the building of Castlerigg stone circle and the trading of Langdale stone axes, the clearing of almost all Lake District forest, and up until today. With luck it will survive the next millenium, but luck is what the Birkrigg woods have run out of. The old trees are romantically falling apart, in the same way as in any other living creature. Eventual death makes space for a young one to fill the gap. And this is where we run into a calamity. There are almost no young ones or seedlings, for these, the next generation, depart in the stomachs of passing sheep.

12th August

The berries of the rowan or mountain ash tree are already turning orange. One may wonder what the hurry is, with other trees such as the lime only now in flower. My guess is that because rowans grow wild on windswept crags on the fells where summers can be short, they get a move on while conditions are good, needing only three to four months for the whole cycle from first leaf to ripe berry. I used to think that dispersal of their berries on the hills was by bird, particularly the flocks of fieldfares which arrive in October. But heavy rain and swollen mountain streams - 'becks' and 'ghylls' - also carry them away and sweep them over waterfalls to lodge in nooks and crannies between rocks where germination can take place.

Meanwhile late summer wildflowers are colouring roadside verges with the blues of scabious, harebells and meadow cranesbill and the purple of knapweeds and betony.

***

Walking in Scotland is one of my favourite pastimes, but then I'm lucky enough to be immune to midges. Some people - including my brother-in-law - refuse to go in summer because of these tiny biting flies or "no-seeums" as Americans aptly call them, which swarm round beauty spots. I must admit there are times when I get fed up with mouthfuls of chewy wings with my sandwiches, so I have been interested to see that this year is turning out to be the 'let's do something about the midges' year.

Two approaches are being tried. The first, which the Scottish Tourist Board is keen on, is to infect the midge with a parasitic worm. The other approach is to rub the oil of the bog myrtle plant on the skin, which is said to repel the midges. Bog myrtle is found wild in Cumbria and Scotland, and I intend to try out its fresh leaves to see if they have any effect*.

* Later that summer I gathered some leaves and mixed them with oil, and applied the aromatic mixture to one leg and not the other. Then I sat reading in a midge-infested woodland clearing. I'm sorry to say that a few midges crawled on both legs, but perhaps it would have been a swarm without the myrtle fragrance. Verdict: open.

19th August

From the evidence left on my garden lawn I knew that a hedgehog was around. He - or she - comes at night, so I took advantage of the full moon last week to go out after dark in search of my visitor. As it turned out, I didn't have far to go and was still alongside the house when I heard scuffling noises in the flower bed. Shining my torch toward the noise revealed a fully grown hedgehog. Did he come for the water dish provided for the birds, I wondered, or for some nice slugs to go with his supper of black beetles?

I went up to him and saw that his spines were now standing up in all directions instead of the backward-smoothed arrangement. The sign of alarm showed that he knew I was there, but his nose and two button eyes remained exposed and he showed no sign of curling into a ball. I went and got some soaked bread and offered it, but he just stood there so I crept away. A few minutes later came happy slurping sounds.

***

A Penrith resident has been bitten by an adder in her garden. It seems most likely that the snake was seeking shade from the sun and was lying partly under a wall or shed. There, overlooked by being in deep shadow, it may have been inadvertently trodden on. Both snake and gardener are still at large.

***

The drought is beginning to affect wild trees on drier soils. Beeches are sporting autumn colours while young ashes go straight to crispy pale green and give up. Oaks seem to be standing up better to the conditions, and are sprouting the characteristic August new growth. This follows a bad start, for this year the oak came out before the ash and some trees were totally blackened by late frosts. The ash waited until the weather was warmer before coming into leaf, and missed the rain. You can't win every time.

26th August

I spent the last hot evening in Derwentwater and on its shore. For company in the water I had a grebe, which let me get quite close but then it dived and reappeared a good fifty yards away. There were swallows skimming the water surface for insects, which were not numerous until suddenly the few yards next to the water's edge was swarming with large black flies. Just as suddenly, ten minutes later, there were none. During the invasion a comical act turned up: a duck foursome paddled smoothly along the edge of the water whilst snapping their heads left, right and up like a clockwork automaton, to grab the flies.

At the shoreline were groups of pied wagtails flitting from rock to rock and some young crows sitting about. One, a rather pathetic character, had a white wing edge on one side. A loud hammering in a hawthorn tree that I thought must be a woodpecker wasn't at all. It was a nuthatch, characteristically upside-down on the branch. The books say that they wedge nuts in bark and then peck them open, which may be what this bird was doing. It certainly was taking the task very seriously and not minding being watched. The nuthatch is a lovely bird, grey and buff-pink and gentle-natured, running along trees upside-down. I particularly like the way my old Field Guide to Birds of Britain and Europe - which I still use - puts it. The italics are theirs: "Climbs trees in short jerks, in any direction including *downwards*". Unfortunately these attractive birds aren't common in north Cumbria, but perhaps the hot summer will encourage them to spread here.

The sunset that evening was wonderful, with the red setting globe in a completely clear sky. A path of gold light crossed the lake against shades of grey water and grey mountain silhouettes. A boat in the distance with its passengers was sharply etched black. Why is it that the photograph of a lifetime always turns up when you haven't got a camera with you? I was sufficiently impressed to return the next evening with camera and a whole new film. Naturally, there was no repeat performance. A band of cloud was approaching and mist could be seen stealing up the sides of mountains.

2nd September

Although the river Eden is exceptionally low, the paths along it are mostly nice and damp. The vegetation in some places is a veritable jungle, where trousers or long socks are needed for pushing through nettles, brambles, sprawling raspberry canes and even the infamous giant hogweed. At one point south of Wetheral young plants of this toxic weed have spread right across the path.

The National Rivers Authority* are trying to keep it under control here as elsewhere, but several plants have got away and their flowering stems can be seen towering ten feet above the undergrowth.

The other intruder, the 'policeman's helmet', or Himalayan balsam, isn't doing particularly well this year, but there's still lots of it and plenty of fat capsules to explode by a gentle squeeze. It's rather a pity that the Latin epithet 'noli-tangere', meaning 'touch-me-not', belongs to the diminutive wild balsam which likewise has explosive fruits. If this little species hadn't grabbed the name first, 'touch-me-not' would have been a good description for the fruits of the policeman's helmet.

One tedious job after a walk in late summer is the removal of seeds from socks. First the hard little pellets of the goosegrass, which I have learned has the wonderful vernacular name of 'sticky Willie'. Then the various curved and hooked forms of agrimony and avens to be brushed off - preferably not over one's own garden - and then the worst. The grass seeds weave themselves prickly-end inward - skinwards - into the very stitches of knitted socks, to emerge just as prickly from the wash.

A solution to terminally offending socks comes from a professional plant-hunter. On returning from a foreign trip he decided that an unwashed pair of his socks was past saving and deserved a decent burial. So he laid them to rest in a seed-tray of compost and kept them watered. Then he counted the kinds of seedlings that grew up.

* The NRA is now part of the Environment Agency

9th September

The other day I picked one of four apples from a young tree. To my horror, that evening the remaining apples all had one bite out of them. In a way, because I always encourage birds and provide some foods for them, I can understand that they can't tell what is a bird table and what is a humans-only food table. It's the timing I can't see as a coincidence. Did they, probably the numerous blackbirds, notice the change in apple number, or did they watch me pick and associate this with the apples being ripe enough for an exploratory bite?

(The following year I sat a white fluffy toy duck in the branches. There were no tastings of the apples at all in its presence)

Lots of wild fruits colour up red, orange or purple when ripe. This makes it easier for us to tell ripeness, and I expect other animals and birds, who also have colour vision, use it to save time too. Purple fruits in the hedges at the moment include elderberries, brambles, sloes and wild damsons.

The ivy is another plant with purple fruits, but its flowering and fruiting are almost six months out of phase with our year. The flowers come out in autumn, and an old wall covered with ivy can be heard from a distance by the buzzing of bees taking nectar. The berries ripen in winter, and becomes a food source for the birds sheltering amongst the tangled stems and evergreen foliage. If you have room in the garden for some old ivy, it is a good plant for helping the birds and other wild life.

16th September

Last weekend our part of the country enjoyed summer weather while most of Britain was under a monsoon. In the Eden Valley there was a hint of approaching autumn, with misty early morning light and a flock of a hundred wild geese occupying a field near Kirkoswald. Spiders' webs of several kinds decorated the vegetation and one or two fungi were growing up. The white stems of the previous day's stinkhorns persisted but the sweetish smell of fresh ones was absent.

The river level on the Eden is still down and a long way below normal, Looking up into the trees reveals just how much higher the level was last winter, as bundles of debris can still be seen trapped among overhanging branches. As I walked along a narrow tributary to the river Eden, a flash of blue shot past and was gone: my very first sight of a kingfisher in north Cumbria.

Other fishing birds are regular sights on the river, and as usual a heron was there. It is rare to walk for any distance on the stretches outside villages without spotting one motionless at the water's edge or standing on the shingle of an island. Several times I have had one rise into the air from almost under my feet - a bit of a shock when those huge grey wings unfold so close.

Once the eye is tuned in to the movement of the river, you start seeing other birds. The dark brown bird flying low over the water is the dipper. It lands on rocks and dips up and down, plump like a robin, exposing a large white bib. It slips rapidly from its rock to the bottom of the stream where it walks around underwater picking up insects.

If you are curious as to what it is finding to eat, turn over a stone or two in the river bed. If it is not too polluted, and if dippers are present the signs are good, there will be plenty of wriggly insects, larvae of mayflies and stoneflies, and little stone huts of caddis larvae.

23rd September

Like thousands of others, I went to the head of Haweswater to see Mardale village and walk on the old roads and over the perfectly-preserved stone bridge. The lake bottom is mud, in various shades of brown, and it has cracked deeply in the manner of deserts. Immense numbers of photographs in the brilliant afternoon sunshine were being taken by visitors, of the near monochrome village framed by scarlet and green rowan trees.

Where the reservoir had been dry for longest, greenstuff had appeared on the mud floor and sheep were grazing. 'Stuff', I thought to myself. That's not very good for someone who's supposed to be a botanist. So I went to look.

It was surprises all the way. Firstly, there was no grass. None. The greenery around the emerged village, in order of numbers, was: water pepper, marsh yellow cress, marsh cudweed, and water purslane. Now water pepper, although a wimpish-looking plant, has a secret weapon. Chewing the leaves is exactly like chewing a chilli pod. Eating them is definitely not recommended. Yet the sheep were not far away and on the lake bed. How was it that they were grazing quietly and not jumping up and down in agony?

When I reached the sheep, on soggy ground with a bright green lawn of vegetation, there still wasn't any grass. None at all from one side of the lake bed to the other. The bright green where I was standing precariously and trying not to sink any deeper into the mud belonged to a spreading rush, the toad rush. It was this that was being grazed by the sheep. Was the water pepper growing here? Yes, abundantly, mixed in with the grazed rushes. The sheep weren't touching it.

30th September

Crab apple trees in the hedgerows are only noticeable twice a year: in spring with flowers on and at the moment as the apples fall off with the wind or rain. Many of these trees are not really wild plants but the result of pips of cultivated trees growing up and reverting to small fruit. However, there are some trees of the real wild apple around, including an exceptionally tall tree at Kelswick, Wythop. The fruits of the original species are round and not elongated, with long stalks, the outline a bit like a large cherry. The best way to spot a tree, as with chestnuts, is to watch the ground rather than looking up.

Archaeology has turned up many records of crab apples being known and eaten in prehistoric times. There are impressions of pips in pottery and whole fruit in waterlogged sites. In 1854 a great drought in Switzerland exposed the beds of lakes and prehistoric villages , dated to 3000 years ago. The lake mud had preserved objects including the food stores and the rubbish perfectly. Amongst many fruits and nuts were whole crab apples and halved ones for drying for winter. But there was something else exposed beside a house wall - a huge mound of cores and skin only. The belief is that the juice was used for cider.

Our cultivated apples have been bred over the centuries by crossing our wild tree with wild species from other parts of Europe and selecting the best offspring. In the seventeenth, eighteenth and nineteenth centuries chance hybridisations led to five or six hundred varieties, preserved and multiplied by sharp-eyed gardeners. In Cumbria those that survive include the Keswick Codling. Unfortunately we have ignored much of this delicious heritage in an age of mass trading, and with very few organisations positively preserving old apple varieties we are losing the raw materials for new delights. The drive towards uniformity is a great pity.

7th October

The year has come round to pond-clearing time, when the mass of vegetation grown in the summer has to be removed before it decays and adds its nutrients to water. This sounds like interfering with a good thing, but a garden pond is too small and too isolated to cope with so much organic material and will become murky and poorer in animal life if left to its own devices. Besides, the compost heap will welcome the wet pile.

A brand-new garden pond will soon attract creatures, from pond skaters arriving in about two days to dragonflies in season. Plants will bring in more creatures as eggs, and even at this time of year turning over a flat pondweed leaf or similar will reveal ovals of jelly which contain eggs of the great pond snail. Submerged rocks are home to many species, including caddis flies with the head and legs poking out from a cylindrical case made of grit, sticks or plant fragments. Water boatmen are underwater bugs which inevitably turn up, about 2 cm long and very aggressive. They 'row' to the surface and down, with lightening-fast reactions if you try to catch one. In my own pond, which is only eighteen months old, another creature has turned up, uninvited, to put me off working on the pond. It is at least two enormous horse leeches, which I was so shocked to see on extracted weed that I stupidly threw the whole lot back in.

***

On a pleasanter note, the hedges are bright with roses bearing very heavy crops of scarlet hips and some hawthorn trees are more red than green. Cotoneasters are being plundered by blackbirds, I'm delighted to say in preference to my remaining apples. Robins are once again making themselves obvious, singing from prominent points on bushes and houses. Unusually amongst garden birds, the male and female are coloured the same and can't be distinguished by appearance. Unusually also, the female owns and defends her own territory until nesting time, so the redbreast you see singing so energetically on that branch may well be female.

14th October

Last Sunday evening we saw clear moonlit skies and warm air, more reminiscent of foreign holidays than of home. Apparently it was caused by the tail of a hurricane passing by to our west on its passage from the Caribbean to oblivion in the arctic. Caught up in the back of the storm was our pocket of hot air which briefly returned us to summer.

Just when it was getting too dark to work outside on that evening, my garden was invaded by a fluttering of brown moths feeding on the buddleia bush and the Mrs Bowles wallflower, that perpetually-flowering purple variety. The moths reminded me of big midges in their movement, keeping hovering even while feeding. I managed to catch one in a jar and put it in the fridge for 5 minutes to slow it down (it recovered perfectly) so I could see the wings. A sharp y-shaped squiggle on each forewing proved it was the Silver Y moth. It has two generations a year, and it was the second which is so numerous on the wing at the moment.

For many plants this is the time of year to shed seeds before winter. Opening fruits can be works of art, and I particularly like the yellow flag or iris whose pods split and roll back in three sections to reveal rows of seeds like stacks of pound coins. Another iris has bright orange seeds. But the prize for sardine-can packing must go to a garden plant, the orange glory vine or Eccremocarpus. Open up the fat pod and it is packed with flat, winged seeds all lying in parallel rows.

21st October

It's fungus time in the woods and hillsides. Until we get some frost there are scores of brightly-coloured toadstools to be found, from purple to orange to various shades of red and purple, and real mushrooms as well.

The most photogenic toadstools are the fly agaric, which has large flat caps of scarlet, with white flecks. At the moment it is common in groups at the edges of light woodland. It is poisonous, but rarely kills people because it looks the part: exotic and dangerous. The real killer is the death cap, which is always fatal even in small parts. Unfortunately it is white and mushroom-shaped. However, it doesn't occur to my knowledge in old pasture, but rather in woodland, and can be distinguished by a white underside to the cap as well as a bulbous base. Real mushrooms have pink undersides turning brown and black as the spores ripen, so underneath a well-grown genuine mushroom you never find it pure white or cream. Except in Chinese restaurants. Chinese mushrooms are a different species and they are brown above and white below, and edible.

The berries on wild trees and garden trees are spectacular this year, with rowans, holly, hawthorn and roses covered in fruit. Discussions abound as to whether the trees 'know' that it's going to be a hard winter, and that's why they have borne so heavily. Personally I don't think trees can foretell the future, but there may be links all the same. Berries, like apples and plums and other fruits are affected by the weather when they come into flower, with high temperatures not only helping the tree but also allowing the pollinating insects to be on the wing longer and visit more flowers.

However, there is a very general rule that the weather stays the same as it has been. This says that if we have had an anticyclone and a hot dry summer, then we will get an anticyclone in the winter, which means cold and dry. So we end up with the same answer: it may be rather cold. Whatever happens, the arguments will doubtless be revived this time next year.

28th October

Autumn colours are not developing greatly this year, but to compensate we still have splashes of colour from wildflowers. Plants which were dying down a month ago have sprouted again with new growth and flowers, particularly the pink herb robert and the yellows of buttercups, hawkweeds and dandelions. The warm wet weather has also prolonged the season for insects, so birds are well-supplied with natural goodies. It isn't yet necessary to feed them on the bird table, but it's a good time for cleaning up and renovating bird tables and feeders.

If, like me, you didn't get round to clearing out the non-hardy plants from the flower garden, you may still be enjoying flowers on tobacco plants, foxgloves, nasturtiums and even poppies, and until last weekend the butterflies were also making the most of them. So were the greenfly.

By chance I had stuck a buddleia cutting in an odd corner during the summer, which grew into a vigorous plant which is still flowering. Only now have I seen that I put the plant in the one spot where the low autumn sun reaches round the house and lights up a small patch out of the general shadow. By accident I have created a very popular feeding place for butterflies and bees late in the day.

Wildlife projects in the garden can be started at this time of the year. Nestboxes can be put up so the birds get used to them, and shelter for all sorts of creatures promoted by allowing tangled vegetation and wood piles to have a spot of their own and not be added to the bonfire. New hedges can be planned with a high proportion of native species, the ones the birds and small creatures can live and feed on.

4th November

Last Sunday, I sat in the sunshine, on an almost-warm rock. The view extended from Scotland to the four plumes of white smoke at Shap and round to the grey shape of Skiddaw towering a thousand feet above me.

It is one of those strange principles that if you are out in the countryside looking for a particular wild plant, and have no luck, you should sit down and get out your refreshments. Between the second cup of coffee and the sandwich, your gaze will suddenly snap out of relaxed mode as you realise that the plant you've almost got your feet on is the one you've been looking for. On Sunday I wasn't looking for anything particular but I did become aware of attractive tufts of grey shoots half an inch tall with bright red blobs at the top. This is a lichen, and these grey and red kinds are Cladonia.

Many lichens don't grow like this at all, but are quite flat, spreading as closely-applied patches on stones. Look closely at a stone wall, the rocks in a field or an old tiled roof, and the surface can be seen not to be the colour of the stone at all but a patchwork of white, grey-white, grey-pink and splashes of yellow-green - all lichens. Thus lichens are a key part of the colour and texture of our landscape. Even the large rocks on the mountainsides, clearly different according to the type of rock, still owe much of their character to the lichens. We are so used to taking this intimate wrapping as the natural and right colour of stone in the landscape that newly eroded rocks can look unnatural.

A consequence of this vegetable wrapping, known to all

hillwalkers, is that grey stones are slippery when wet. The lichen absorbs water to become jelly-like and suddenly there is no friction between boot and surface. Will this occur on the newly-repaired stone paths? Will lichens cover them in time and render them slippery too?

Fortunately, lichens grow slowly. Their growth rates are well-studied, not so much by putting a ruler across a patch every year but by the realisation that gravestones in church-yards provide known earliest dates when their lichen cover started to grow.

11th November

Thirlmere has never been one of my regular walking haunts, I think because I used to associate it in my mind with the dark barrier of trees along the main road. However, this year I have got to know the far side, west of the lake, and have found it delightful. There are many footpaths from the car parks on the back road, varying from waymarked forest trails to the high fell path to Watendlath, and now there is a public footpath the whole length of the lake, in woodland which is open and sunlit.

Beneath the trees along this path are wildflowers, still blooming in the mild weather, and enormous toadstools. In the trees I saw squirrels and numerous groups of small birds, while just above the top of the forest, a thousand feet up the hillside, there were flocks of fieldfares pausing in the rowan trees before flying on south.

On the road near Armboth I came across a signpost directing me to the 'Giant Tree'. It led me up some steps into the forest, along and up bit more until the forest opened out. Ahead was a huge grey tree trunk of a silver fir. Up the trunk, and up for 141 feet, the eye eventually reaches the top. I was surprised to read on the plaque that the tree was only planted in 1821.

Height records for trees was a new subject to me, but a booklet 'Ancient, Interesting and Unusual Trees of Cumbria' from Cumbria Broadleaves reveals that Cumbria holds a number of records. The Christmas tree - Norway spruce - with the largest girth anywhere in the British Isles is at Lingholm Gardens, near Keswick, and Lingholm also have a 145 foot silver fir. The tallest western white pine, at 131 feet, is at Patterdale Hall, and a runner-up for the tallest lime tree in the British Isles, also at 131 feet, is at Hutton in the Forest

18th November

A reader of these Notes remarked to me that I am lucky to live surrounded by so much nature. 'Yes', indeed, I replied, I am. But also 'no', nature is not confined to my garden and walking areas! It's all around. Despite less space and scope for wildlife in a built-up town centre, there will still be something to see even in the middle of Penrith.

Having made this prediction, I wandered down into the town, fingers crossed that there would be something around in the way of plants or birds. I needn't have worried about birds: the noise of starlings and sparrows was obvious. With them in the trees were blackbirds, robins, jackdaws and chaffinches, all quite unafraid of passers by. On house roofs were two kinds of seagull, the herring gull which wears an arrogant expression and squawks loudly and the smaller black-headed gull. This has no black head at this time of year, the head becoming white except for a dark spot behind the eye. Moving to the more twitchy birds, a high-pitched squeaking came from a flock of eight goldfinches feeding on dandelion seeds (good for them, there'll be less coming up as weeds next year). Bluetits hopped around tree branches, often upside down, scouring the bark for insects. In all, the total numbers of bird species I saw along a mile of roads was eleven.

At the top of Friargate in Penrith a mass of ivy was flowering, and despite being sodden from the rain was attracting honeybees, wasps and flies. My next exploration was the walls around St Andrew's churchyard. Here delicate maiden-hair spleenwort ferns with black midribs to the fronds were spreading from crevices in the vertical stone walls. A few plants of ivy-leaved toadflax grew in the larger gaps, and the surface of damper patches of wall was green with mosses of several kinds, including the wall moss with a silvery sheen to its green. This and others had plenty of brown, stalked capsules. While these contain spores and not seeds, for mosses go back in history long before seeds and flowers existed, the method of dispersal is just like that of a poppy with its pepper-pot seed-head. In dry weather the capsule lid opens up and spores are shaken into the air and ultimately to fall to the ground where they will germinate.

25th November

One of my favourite sights in the low yellow light at this time of year is the peeling bark of a birch tree. Seen against the light, on a slender copper-coloured trunk, the translucent bark peelings glow like fire. A bit of gentle tidying-up and pulling off these loose outer layers doesn't harm the tree, and will reveal the fresh bark that feels wonderfully smooth to the touch. The papery layers that peel off are strong and waterproof, and have been used in many countries to make utensils and boats and roofing.

Even the individuals that are brownest when young gradually acquire a white trunk with age, as reflected in the name 'silver birch'. However, pure white trunks on the youngest trees are a characteristic of a garden variety of birch, a small group of which can be seen on the pedestrian area of Carlisle. This variety was brought into cultivation from western India and Pakistan, and because, so the argument goes, any competent person can distinguish it from the silver birch, it qualifies as a species in its own right. It was named *Betula jaquemontii*. Then along came the next classifier, who saw that all sorts of transitions between white-when-young and brown-when-young trees existed in the Himalayas, and the species was despatched (with extreme prejudice). We must call it *Betula utilis*, the same name as our wild silver birch and all the Asian miscellany.

However, I imagine that the next classifier to come along will find that there's something unique about the hairs on the leaf veins of the snow-white plants, and they can be a species after all. Meanwhile, when I order one from the nursery, I'll make sure I get the right tree by asking for 'the one that used to be called jacquemontii'.

There isn't room to mention all the interesting coloured and textured bark to be seen, from Eucalyptus to Japanese maples to the strawberry tree. The ultimate in 'feelie-bark' belongs to two unrelated species: *Stewartia koreana* and *Prunus serrula*. These have gold to rosewood-coloured bark, polished and metallic in texture and very very touchable.

2nd December

Beaches and lakeshores tempt me to potter about, looking for glowing pebbles which lose their magic when they dry, and for treasures in the drift debris at high water mark.

Last Saturday I walked along part of the Cumbria Coastal path from Silloth towards Carlisle. I found it a most attractive walking route, with the bonus of a dry and largely sunny day while in the distance Skiddaw hid under rain-clouds. Beachcombing produced pink granite pebbles and fresh indigo-and-pearl mussel shells.

Part of the path follows sand dunes with gorse bushes, in flower, and a scrub of the burnett rose, a plant which gardeners have co-opted for informal hedging. Several rose plants had new white flowers, as did thrift, sea aster and some handsome dandelions. Beach-combing at the sea's edge yielded pink granite pebbles.

The coastal path goes to the very edge of the Solway estuary, with an option to follow a line of posts across the grass of the saltmarshes. This proved quite an adventure, because the marked route is underneath the sea at high tide and the traverse must be carefully planned. Even so, water was seeping or pouring up the creeks barring the way every hundred yards or so. Most of the party ended with one or two wet feet, as jumping the creeks seemed preferable to tackling the deep grey mud. The tide came in fast, from all directions at once, or so it seemed, and reminded me of a paragraph from J. M. Synge's 'The Aran Islands':

"A man who is not afraid of the sea will soon be drownded", he said, "for he will be going out on a day when he shouldn't. But we do be afraid of the sea, and we do only be drownded now and again."

All went well with our crossing, and we emerged via a particularly luscious stretch of mud onto proper dry land again with golden grass and hedgerow trees.

9th December

I never get tired of the colours of our winter landscape. Earlier this week I took the long way by car from Keswick to Carlisle, past Mosedale to Caldbeck, and paused for a while on the open grassland near Calebreck. The sun shone from a blue sky onto a tapestry of greens, rusts and straw colours. Each kind of plant was a different green, from the bright green of sheep-grazed grass to the straws and reds of old sedge and grass leaves, to the green and yellow of gorse bushes in flower.

Winter hedges and trees, too, were far from dull. Beech and oak trees still had individuals clothed in gold leaves, and beech hedges keep the old leaves through the winter. Roadside willows bore a sprinkling of yellow leaves and small patches of bright red rose hips added colour. Large tree trunks, if looked at twice, weren't brown or grey but a patchwork of silvery bark, green moss, grey lichen, often a patch of ivy, and green powdery algae.

Woodland trees, when seen as a mass against a contrasting background, can be seen to be different colours even when bare. At the top of the trees the fine shoots and next-year's buds have a distinct colour, red in beeches, pink-red in birch and pale fawn in ash. Hazel trees are loaded with blue-grey (or would 'sea-green' better describe the colour?) catkins ready to emerge in the early spring. I've never seen such masses of catkins as on the trees this autumn. Will other kinds of tree also have an exceptional load of flower buds?

As I approached Carlisle, the sun and then the light went out. Curtains of snow hanging down from the sky were a sensational view one moment, and around me the next. With all these quick changes in the weather, it's just as well that most trees 'shut up shop' for the duration of the winter and don't get tempted to put out leaves in a sunny intermission.

16th December

A walk up Beacon Hill at the back of Penrith has the pleasure of a dry path underfoot. For much of the fenced section, the sandstone rock is at the surface. The walker treads on the bare bones of the earth.

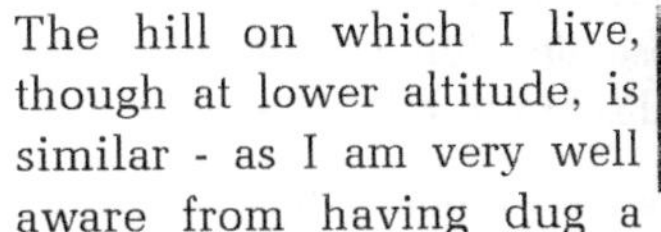

The hill on which I live, though at lower altitude, is similar - as I am very well aware from having dug a four-foot-deep pond. It was sand all the way down to sandstone, where thistles still rooted as far as I went. But to reach Beacon Hill I have to cross a band of clay, which stops rainwater draining away, and gives rise to springs where water passing down through the sandstone suddenly meets this impermeable layer.

This clay, now exposed in huge bands by house-building operations, is mixed with rocks and sand and must be boulder clay left by a glacier flowing through Penrith during the last Ice Age.

Glaciers moving over the whole region would also explain the types of stones surfacing in our gardens which are definitely 'offcomers', such as some very heavy rounded blue pieces.

The best clay has been used for hundreds of years in the Penrith area for making pottery. Bits of very old glazed pots turn up in town gardens, from ancient potteries which haven't so far been precisely located.

Back on the path up the Beacon, I noticed that I was walking on fallen leaves of the sweet chestnut tree. This tree was brought to Britain by the Romans, for timber for rot-resistant poles and fence-posts rather than for the nuts, of which few grow to proper size and ripeness here. Perhaps it's surprising that we get any to ripen, as the tree pushes its luck by flowering in July. The conspicuous unpleasant-smelling yellow catkins carry male flowers, at the base of which is a group of three females. These develop into the familiar painfully-prickly green capsules around the chestnuts.

The books tell me that the flowers are pollinated by insects, which would explain the smell, and also explain how it is that the female flowers get pollinated when they open after the male ones on the same branch have died: different trees are at slightly different stages, and insects can convey pollen from one to another. I also learnt that the sweet chestnut is a close relative of the beech tree. I'd never thought about this, but three beech nuts in an opened warty capsule are indeed on the same pattern as the chestnut.

23rd December

Greystoke Forest has been opened up to the public with the provision of two well-marked walking trails, shown on a map at the entrances. The longer trail is five or six miles, and the shorter one and a half miles. The latter, a circuit from Millfield Lodge, attracted me because there was a tarn or pond marked on the route.

From the road it isn't obvious how open and varied the plantations are inside, nor that one can see out as far as the mountains in the background. On the short route there is a section between walls of dense dark conifers but then the path emerges into an old pine wood, where sunlight reaches the ground and grasses and flowers grow. The pond or tarn is here, containing a large clump of bulrushes with brown fruiting stems. The banks of the pond are clay, so the first thing I did was to have a good look for footprints before adding my own, but there weren't any, not even of the abundant deer in this forest.

The pondwater is beautifully clear, but too cold at this time of year for much life. Even turning over pondweed leaves revealed nothing, but then I spotted some empty caddis cases in floating debris. Caddis flies spend their juvenile stage under water, in a 'house' around their bodies. This case is built of local materials, and different varieties of caddis live in different habitats and make different cases. These particular discarded cases were patchwork quilts of reed and horsetail stems in various shades of green, the whole structure only an inch long. I knew that if I looked under submerged stones in one of the rocky streams I would find another kind of caddis case, knobbly and made of tiny pebbles. Indeed there were, with about one in three stones bearing a caddis case. Some were still occupied, and warmth and patience succeeded in getting a little insect head to emerge.

Around the pond were fallen trees quietly decaying while supporting ferns. mosses, fungi, spiders, beetles and snails. The ground between was marshy, with Sphagnum moss, and I was delighted to see one of my favourite plants, the marsh cinquefoil. This is a tall, red-flowered relative of the common yellow cinquefoils, and reasonably frequent in Cumbria. It can be sought in areas of abundant vegetation bordering lakes, just at the point where you start to get water coming in over the top of your boots.

30th December 1995

With temperatures of -15 degrees in Penrith, and plants looking very sorry for themselves, the idea of global warming having an effect on the wild plants of our countryside seems academic. I imagine I'm not alone in being more concerned over whether my own garden perennials are still alive after this week. However, researchers at the Institute of Terrestrial Ecology are taking a serious look at the possible losses of wild plants and spread of others should the climate warm up.

One way of protecting plants during our local deep freeze is to cover them with fleece or straw, or leave the shelter of their own dead stems and leaves in place. Bracken keeps itself cosy this way: all those russet patches of dead fronds on the fellsides can be thought of as blankets over the underground buds which would die at the limits of their range without this protection.

Bracken grows in most countries of the world, and is increasing elsewhere just as in Britain. It is believed that the spread on open hillsides is not from spores making brand-new plants but by vegetative advance of the underground stems. Our Cumbrian fellside plants may be a thousand years old, or maybe go back to the first acidification of the soil twice as long ago. Because bracken is already a nuisance in harbouring sheep ticks and under suspicion that the spores could cause cancer in humans, further spread as a result of climatic improvement isn't welcome.

Nothing much eats it. The leaves or fronds contain several poisons, from cyanide in the young tender fronds to carcinogens, substances which promote cancer in animals, in all parts of the plant. Other nasties include a substance which destroys bone marrow in cattle and an enzyme which kills animals by knocking out a necessary food component. Interestingly, the micro-organisms that live in the stomachs of ruminant animals like sheep and cattle can supply the missing nutrient, so ruminants can eat a certain amount of bracken. Pigs and horses on the other hand are susceptible.

Bracken used to be a valuable resource and was sold for excellent compost, used as animal bedding and as a tolerable fuel. Cutting the grown fronds did weaken the plants and restrain their spread, and 'bracken-bashing' is still the best way of control. If global warming does help the spread, we may find ourselves mulching our gardens with bracken instead of peat next century.

1996

6th January

My pond, like all water in the open, is deeply frozen. Quite by chance I discovered a way to make a hole through the ice and satisfy my curiosity about how thick the ice was. Certainly too thick for me to excavate or otherwise make any impression on. Using force was out of the question as hammering ice creates shock-waves and would harm the frogs and other creatures that I hoped were happily sleeping away the winter at the bottom..

Some while ago a twelve-inch plastic flower-pot had blown in and had been floating upright with just the rim above water. As the thaw began the black pot loosened itself a little and I managed to haul it to the side and out, complete with its core of ice which I tipped out onto the lawn and fetched a measuring tape. The answer was that the ice was a good five inches thick. And where the pot had floated I now had a beautiful round hole, as neat as if it had been cut with a giant pastry cutter, right through five inches of ice. The pot is going to go back to the pond in due course to be ready for the next freeze-up.

During the coldest weather a large birch tree in Penrith, full of dangling seed tassels, was host to a twittering flock of linnets. Underneath, blackbirds picked over piles of dead leaves and mossy earth. I seem to be seeing more male blackbirds than female out feeding - coincidence perhaps, or the males might be bolder.

Chaffinches and greenfinches are visiting our bird tables in town. They feed peacefully in groups, unlike the starlings who appear to waste energy by attacking whichever of the group has started on a morsel of food rather than find their own piece. The seagulls, descending in a great flurry of white wings like snow, are even worse. They don't get any chance to eat what they find but must snatch a piece of food and fly off, hotly pursued by screaming companions. Then they return, and line up along nearby roofs to wait for the next excitement.

13th January

Beatrix Potter's keen observation of wild plants and animals comes across in the credibility of her characters and the settings they inhabit. Even the starting point for the Story of the Flopsy Bunnies, that they ate lettuce and became drowsy, is based on the scientific fact that lettuce contains a sedative drug, although not enough in modern crisp lettuce to be noticeable.

What I didn't know, and am just catching up on, is that Beatrix Potter's childrens' books were her second venture into illustrated writing. Her first was the study of small plants and creatures of the countryside. This was true original research, into how and where creatures lived and their detailed structure. She painted accurate yet attractive illustrations of spiders, bats, lizards and amongst plants particularly toadstools, mosses and lichens. She wrote about the colour and texture of lichens coating trees and walls, and curiosity led to putting her mind to work to discover what sort of plant they were.

Without formal training in science, she had a natural gift for observation, read widely and visited the Natural History Museum at South Kensington when in London during the winter seasons. She made contact with scientific societies, where papers on plant structure and classification were published. In time she had worked out that lichens were a very odd kind of plant indeed, composed of algae and fungi. She tried to tell the scientific world but unfortunately, although she was absolutely right, no-one took her seriously.

The paintings of small plants and animals from this period of her life have found a home in a new conservation guide. Flora for Fauna lists the plants which can be grown to feed and shelter wild animals, and it was felt that Beatrix Potter would have been happy to help this project. The guide is still being added to, in the annual flowers section, following trees, shrubs and perennials. Examples from it are hawthorn hedges which shelter scores of birds and insect species as well as producing berries, and sunflowers which have nectar for lacewings and hoverflies plus seeds. I can certainly vouch for birds liking sunflower seeds, as I watch the greenfinches and chaffinches eating their way through the seeds, neatly shedding the husk and swallowing the nut inside. Sparrows, tits and starlings also know the trick, but I haven't seen it demonstrated by large birds.

20th January

Spring seemed to have arrived for a day as I stood in late-afternoon sunshine in Whinlatter forest, overlooking Bassenthwaite Lake. The trees around the car park were larch, the bare branches dotted with oval cones. This species sheds its needles in autumn just like a broadleaved tree, being responsible for the golden drifts on paths and lakesides before Christmas.

The ground here, unlike that under mature spruce forests which are evergreen, was open to the winter sunlight and covered over with grass and other green plants. The little trefoil leaves of wood-sorrel were scattered abundantly amongst carpets of moss. Its flowers, delicate nodding white bells, will appear in May and last in shady places until autumn. Wood-sorrel doesn't look remotely like its namesake, the sorrel used in cooking, but the leaves have the same acid taste. Botanically it is an *Oxalis*, a wild member of the garden and greenhouse plants of the same name and the same clover-like leaves.

I was surprised to find a number of fungi flourishing after the recent deep freeze. Wood woolly-foots (? woolly-feet), brown toadstools with a centrally-dented cap and fuzzy bottom of the stalk, were fresh, and so were a lot of the tiny fairy clubs, densely-branched cream or white bunches on the ground. Darker, sheltered corners of the wood, produced the bright yolk-yellow stagshorn fungus, one to two inches high, growing out of rotted-down timber.

Clumps of green ferns were generally the largest plants under the trees, and in the realm of ferns they stand out at this time of year compared with the brown crispy leaves of bracken, parsley fern of mountain screes and others which die back with no green above ground. The evergreen kinds include spleenworts on walls, the polypody on tree trunks, and the large clumps of *Dryopteris*, or 'Male Fern' on woodland floors. The fronds of the latter are up to two feet long, and on the undersides the brown dots of the spore sacs can be seen. When the spring really comes, they - like all ferns - will unroll new curled leaves for the new season.

3rd February

A week ago, the sky was thick with white snowflakes and the grey-white shapes of seagulls. When it cleared, I put some more food out for the birds, but placed it at the corner of two walls and a fence where the voracious seagulls would find it difficult to fly.

Immediately a row of starlings appeared on the fence, each just beyond touching distance of its neighbours. Beaks were wiped, and mouthfuls of snow eaten. Something looked different in their faces: no eyes. The eyes were sunken in raised feathers and looked shut, even during the squawking and feeding on the ground.

I was beginning to recognise one or two black-headed gull individuals, in particular one with a heavy black bar down its face and a black border on its tail: a youngster. Its usual companion had the merest dot of black behind the eye and a white tail. Soon the black marks will extend to the full black face for summer.

These two spent most of the time looking elegant and remote on top of a roof, but occasionally made an attempt to land in the middle of the starling crowd to grab a piece of food. To get down from the sky they hovered with legs dangling, tail fanned open, and once in a while succeeded in a momentary touch-down. The other gulls, common gulls, left this enclosed corner alone and continued to circle the wide open spaces.

Do the larger birds, I wonder, smell food or do they come along and investigate anything looking different on their 'patch'? I recall many occasions of eating sandwiches on the fells and seeing a raven come past and circle once or twice, as if satisfying its curiosity. Once in mid Wales, in the middle of a vast desolate moor, I cooked soup for lunch and looked up to find a red kite above my head. I'm convinced it came to investigate.

While we wait to see how many more snowy spells this winter has in store, I came across this bit of fun from an eighteenth century poet:

Snowy, Flowy, Blowy,

Showery, Flowery, Bowery,

Hoppy, Croppy, Droppy,

Breezy, Sneezy, Freezy.

'The Twelve Months', by George Ellis.

10th February

Snowdrop is a lovely name for a lovely flower, the perfect white blooms defying the frost and wind. It seems immune to the tearing floodwaters of riversides, as along the river Petteril north of Wreay where clumps emerge from the matted debris of wood and leaves. The petals don't seem to bruise, something I was about to experiment on when a foot of snow dropped out of the sky. At least the snow should provide a good blanket to protect the emerging flowers and plants from the frost, and they should be in fine form as soon as the thaw arrives.

I have been told that there are a dozen waxwings in Penrith, feeding on Cotoneaster berries. I'd love to see this reputedly tame bird with its pink crest and colourful yellow and red-splashed tail. More abundant are fieldfares on berries in the town. In close-up this is a handsome bird with grey head and a touch of russet about both its speckled breast and its back. Like the waxwing, it only visits us for the winter and then flies back to northern Scandinavia and north-eastern Europe.

I have access at home to weather satellite photographs like those used on the television weather forecasts, and they've become a bit of an addiction over the last few days. General photographs are freely available to the public from a number of satellites travelling over the earth and easily printed from the Internet to make a permanent record of interesting days. New photographs are added to the public collection about every two hours, and by using infra-red images this includes night-time as well. Just as on the television pictures - though not in colour - the masses of cloud can be seen, changing shape and direction, coming our way or not.

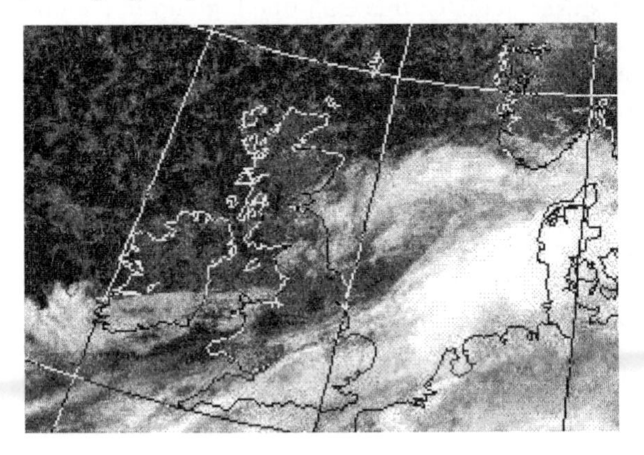

From the great height of the satellites, pictures encompass all the region from Greenland to Scandinavia to north Africa. The striking thing to me has been this grand scale on which patterns develop, and the insignificance and vulnerability of a small piece of land on the edge of this great playing field of the elements. For example this week a thin streamer of cloud extended from Greenland to Norway, and our 'snow-machine' was part of a three-thousand-mile-long white band. I'm no longer surprised that we are in the middle of winter one day, spring the next and then back to winter.

17th February

Water, water everywhere. All that snow, and the hours spent digging out paths and roads, and on the first free day at the weekend there's little left but slush. Actually, this isn't true high up in the hills, as I discovered by driving over Hartside four days later. Through the blizzard my headlights picked out huge walls of solid snow, fortunately not melting all over the road.

Down in warmer climes, the road from Pooley Bridge to Patterdale along the side of Ullswater was a succession of pools, patterned rivulets and fords. Some of these were deep where newly-created rivers crossed the road on their way to the lake. Footpaths were sodden or hijacked by bubbling streams, and higher up disappeared into wet snow. Fell-walking, and Helvellyn in particular, looked somewhere between pointless and impossible. So what does one do on a wet day?

The map suggested the answer: waterfalls. Aira Force was nearby and the sight of so much water running down the hills suggested that the falls would be worth seeing. And so they were, with the noise and the spray extending beyond the gorge. At the main fall, clouds of billowing spray rose upwards across the trees and fell slowly in drifting curtains. The water itself, thundering down, was off-white with eroded peat and travelling very fast indeed.

Back at the car park, we were accosted in the nicest way by a robin and then chaffinches, and then a very bedraggled wet bluetit. All took food (corners of sandwiches) from the hand and flew off to a safe distance before returning for seconds and thirds. After a while there were four bluetits (one wet and three dry), a pair of blackbirds, and suddenly not one but two orange breasts, and a sharp scuffle and chase under the car.

Peace briefly returned, but a rook materialised out of nowhere, and then jackdaws staked out the overhanging branches. Soon this heavy brigade was fighting amongst itself in the air for any scraps, and the sandwich-sharing service was withdrawn.

24th February

Derwentwater on Wednesday was calm after the recent storms. The ice has gone, save for sheltered inlets and around reed beds. As the water level is now lower than when the surface froze, thin sheets of ice are suspended in air looking rather like panes of glass in a greenhouse. The sheets were patterned with silver lines in circles and ovals in the manner of contour lines on a map, and protruding stones were ringed by silver-edged holes.

Near the shoreline below Great Wood is a group of mature pine trees. I've always privately thought of them as the 'chocolate pines', on account of the colour of their bark. On summer evenings this shore picks up the last of the sun before it sets, and the treetrunks glow a pinky-brown that seems to me to be the colour of milk chocolate.

As in so many stands of mature trees, all the individuals are about the same age and there is no natural regeneration. I was delighted therefore to see some plastic tubes where the National Trust has been planting young pine trees. Whether or not the seed for the new trees came from this site I haven't yet been able to find out.

I walked back to Great Wood up a stream where icicles still clung to rocks and clumps of grass overhanging the water had thick coats of ice. Then, as I emerged into the open and the sunlight, snowflakes began once again to drift down from the thickening cloud.

On the corner of the exit road from the National Trust car park at Great Wood is a massive Douglas Fir. I must have driven past it on many occasions without noticing it, until a branch fell off recently which attracts attention. The rugged trunk, despite the great thickness of the bark, is showing stretch marks running vertically where the outer layers are being pulled apart to accommodate an increase in girth. This is the sort of tree to admire on other peoples' estates and to be thankful that the previous owners of one's home didn't fancy on the front lawn.

2nd March

Beachcombing isn't just for the seaside. I discovered this when I went out for a walk along the river Eamont after the water level had risen and fallen over a few days. The effect was as if the tide had been in and out at the seaside: a drift-line of debris at the high water line and sparkling-clean grass and sand to the water's edge. Besides being washed, the grass looked exactly as if it had been combed, all the leaves aligned parallel to the river.

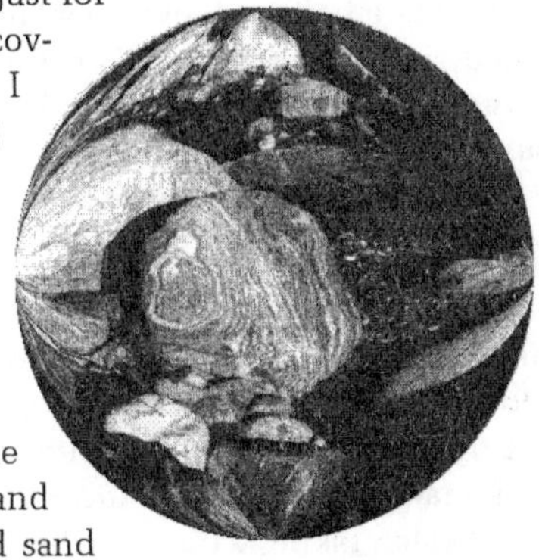

The pebbles on the Eamont's bed are a mixed lot, with red sandstone and grey limestone plus 'foreigners' of various sorts - rocks brought here in glacial boulder clay. I spent a while hunting amongst the wet stones for the ultimate attractive pebble to add to the collection on the mantelpiece. The choice included smooth ovals with bands of different colour, brightly-coloured pink and purple chunks and occasional crystals of white quartz.

Focusing on ground-level, I started to see drifts of fine sand mixed with bits of plant and animal material. The prettiest collections of debris were just shells, tiny fragile snails and cockle-like bivalves up to a third of an inch across. Depressions at the side of rocks gathered more washed-up material - a half shell of a hazel nut, seeds of alder and hog-weed, and horn-like caddis cases made of tiny sand-grains cemented together. My old 'Observer's Book of Pond Life' says that the adult caddis fly of this species is known as the 'Welshman's Button'. Another investigation to be stored for when time allows!

Rabbit-holes in the bank puzzled me at first. The holes were near the top, with two feet of sheer cliff below them and a foot of drop from the field level. I tried to imagine bunnies taking a running leap up into the entrance, but the real explanation must be that the cliff has been cut back by the floodwater, taking with it the 'front doors' of the rabbit burrows.

9th March

I went out to the garden now it's clear of snow, to see how many plants survived the extreme cold of January. Surprisingly, there was only one obvious casualty, a number of Hebe species. They had looked fine a month ago but suddenly collapsed this week, so it's clearly too soon to start counting chickens, as it were.

Getting down to some gentle weeding showed exactly which plants had come through unscathed and were coming into flower: hairy bittercress, dandelion, chickweed and other weeds. I've learnt that the bittercress needs to be pulled up now before the flowers set into seed. One reason I have so much of it coming up is that last year I pulled up old flowering plants, each throwing a shower of seeds to the ground as I did so.

I had been planning a bit of experimentation on snowdrops since marvelling at their presence on river banks recently battered by floodwater. Firstly, I held down a flower under the pounding of water from my highest-pressure tap. No effect. A week later that flower is indistinguishable from others in a vase with it.

Something more severe was needed. I put a shoot with a flower through the washing machine. The flower didn't like that, and came out like a wet tissue. The leaves, though, are alive two weeks later. That's enough destruction for a nice flower: I conclude that the snowdrop is just plain tough.

16th March

On occasions over the last three decades when I welcomed a quiet, solitary walk I found this in the path from the Newlands valley to Buttermere along Rigg Beck and Sail Beck. I remember the path years ago as a thin grassy depression on the ground. Now it is hard-edged and generally eroded to a stony base, showing that other walkers know of it. Nevertheless, I've not yet coincided with another person.

Last week I started up the valley on a sunny day with the gorse bushes in flower and the beck bubbling noisily away beside the path. It's not what one could call spectacular scenery, but the path has definite objectives: a boggy col, the next valley, and the descent into civilisation.

Soon after the start the Birkrigg oakwoods come into view above, clinging to the screes below Causey Pike. I visited the woods last in the full heat of the summer, so it seemed a good idea to have a look in winter.

The ground under the trees was still soft and green, with grass and moss, and much evidence of sheep sheltering there. The twisted trunks - for the trees are multistemmed rather than branched - had overcoats of moss up to six feet above the ground, some of which was peeling off in large pieces to reveal the odd silvery bark of these trees. I was delighted to see an acorn on the ground, with its scarlet root tip heading down into the soil. According to the 'New Naturalist' book on the Lake District, these woods are thought to be too high up to produce acorns every year.

Being more than half-way up Causey Pike by now, I climbed up to the top (not a way I recommend in the slightest, except perhaps for the fine bilberries at the right season). It was a different world on the ridge with snow and ice coating the slopes out of the sun. Being more in tune with greenery and flowers on this occasion, I turned down into the Coledale valley and along to Braithwaite, turning the walk into a circle. Crocuses and irises were flowering in gardens, and behind a memorial seat on the way into the village was a clump of primroses in full flower.

23rd March

A drift of grey down on the grass led me to a trail of strong grey and white feathers: the wing feathers of a heron. How had it come to fall onto the field? Could it possibly still be alive? The scattering of feathers led to the bank of the River Eamont and there, in the shallow water, a heron was standing. Could it possibly be? But no, this one rose up with its tremendous wings perfectly intact and moved a little way upstream.

Rooks were busy flying from their rookery to the river to collect nest material. Their supply was the piles of woody debris swept down the river, caught up against tree roots and now high and dry above the low river level. I watched them choose sticks: highly branched bits of alder were popular, while others, perhaps still building the foundations, went for straight sticks several times longer than the width of the nest.

Have you ever looked at something and not seen it? I was out for a walk and bit of fresh air in a village, admiring ferns on a damp stone wall. To be honest, it was a grey day and a gloomy country lane without anything to catch the eye apart from the rows of ferns. Even so, an untidy clump of bleached grass and moss spoiled their symmetrical pattern. Then, in front of my eyes, the grass changed into a curtain in front of a moss sphere. The ball of moss had a circular hole near the top. I was looking at a perfect nest, from last year, probably belonging to the wrens which flit along hedgerows warning the world of your arrival with robin-like tic-tic's.

I examined the rest of the wall, and particularly the patches of thicker moss. Sure enough, I had been missing things, like two more nests snuggled into the moss. What a contrast they were from the rooks' bundles of draughty twigs, these nests walled and roofed with thick soft moss.

Will the birds return to nest this year, despite cars and people inches away from their homes? I'll be going back to see - from a distance this time.

PS. Not long after this was written the wall was stripped of all moss and ferns, and the great sandstone blocks of the cap were spirited away.

30th March

Wainwright called the traverse of High and Low Rigg above St John's-in-the-Vale a 'splendid little expedition admirably suited to old and rickety fell walkers'. I wonder if reading this has deterred the less rickety out of pride in their fitness or youth? If it has it's a pity. The ridges are delightful miniature mountains, and there are steep bits, rocky bits, boggy bits, streams, tarns in abundance and open views.

The high tarns are a wonderful sight in summer when the bog bean produces its pink frilly flowers. It isn't actually a bean at all, botanically, but a gentian with leaves a bit reminiscent of those of the broad bean, divided into three: hence the Latin name of *Menyanthes trifoliata*. The plant only thrives in acidic water like these bog-encircled tarns, and won't grow for me in alkaline Penrith soil.

I visited Low Rigg last weekend with the objective of finding if frogspawn had arrived up in the hills. I've had reports of frogs dying in January due to the low temperatures, but they've survived at Tewet Tarn. I couldn't find a single frog, but the marshy inflow and outflow streams had plenty of spawn. The tarn proper had no spawn, and as in summer it wriggles with massed tadpoles, I imagine they move in when it warms up. As usual, there were patches left in temporary puddles which were now drying out, so I moved this spawn to permanent water. Sounds easy? Imagine a 5-litre pan full of jelly just beginning to set. Your task is to lift out the entire contents without breaking it, with just your hands.

Fortunately it was a beautiful day for messing around in water, with a skylark singing and six buzzards circling high over Latrigg. A pair of coot were swimming on the tarn, with an occasional chirrup and splashes as they dived. The air at last was still and bright, with the luminous quality of summer days. And how did I manage the frogspawn? With the bag liner from my rucksac. I slid the spawn in, moved to water and let it slide out. Hands alone are not enough.

6th April

From Penrith the mountains both to the east and west, to the Pennines and to the Lake District, are especially clear because of the amount of snow still remaining. My own view of Blencathra will disappear when the trees come into leaf, but the buds are hardly moving at the moment. Under the trees, however, wild flowers are coming through.

The dog's mercury is the first new growth and flower after winter on many woodland floors, and as such I'm always pleased to see it. It's a reassurance that the year is moving forward and that other flowers will follow. Apart from that, the plant is not attractive to look at with coarse green leaves and tiny green flowers. As far as I know no-one has attempted to exploit its very early flowering and develop a garden variety from it.

Dog's mercury has one odd feature: when dried, the plant turns blue. I knew this a long time ago when making pressed plant collections for school, but assumed that I had failed to dry this one properly. Now I know that it won't stay green.

Much prettier flowers are now on the woodland floor, making the most of the short period between winter with light but no warmth and summer with warmth and no light. A walk through woods along the river Eden produced clumps of primroses in sunny spots, with masses of cream flowers. Amongst the carpet of dead leaves the divided leaves of wood anemone were unfolding. The stem straightens from the 'ostrich' position of head in the soil to upright, when the flower bud at the top of the stem opens into the delicate pink-tinged 'windflower'.

Banks at the edge of the wood had the darker, shiny yellow flowers of the celandine and the pebble banks near the water the soft dandelion-like flowers of the coltsfoot. Both are weeds in gardens, but like the blue forget-me-not I allow them to grow for their early flowers. Then they repay the hospitality by spreading all over the garden.

13th April

There's good news and bad news this week. The bad news is the stealing of a rare wild plant from a quarry on Beacon Edge. The good news is the report that a pair of golden eagles is breeding.

The sight of these great birds soaring over the Lake District inspires and gives pleasure to many people. Yet there are individuals intent on wiping out this pleasure and heritage, as well as the birds themselves. By taking and killing the eggs they would steal not just eggshells, not just the future of the birds - for without new generations they are doomed - but also people's happiness in this local success to set against so many wildlife catastrophes. The loss of the eggs would take away the joy of following the chicks growing up, the climate of hope for their future, and the parents' tranquillity, all for the private possession of some empty shells.

Egg collecting was once a common pastime, but interest has moved to watching living creatures rather than museum specimens, thanks to television programmes, wild-life centres, guided walks and books. There is more money, too, nowadays, from living creatures than from dead, via marketable activities such as photography, writing and tourism. Plants have had their own shift in emphasis, away from collecting pressed herbarium specimens and towards enjoying living plants.

Unfortunately there are still plant lovers who seem to think they're in the last century, when expeditions went abroad to scour the countryside for potential garden plants. Nowadays botanical expeditions only collect in co-operation with the host country, in limited amounts, and donate knowledge and plants in return. I hate to think what would happen to a visitor in China today who stopped their car, jumped out with a trowel and cardboard box and proceeded to dig up roadside rarities.

Friends in Watermillock tell me they see people stopping to dig up the primroses opposite their drive, and if they protest they're told it's none of their business. Actually, that's not so. It's against the law to dig up wild flowers. And usually pointless, as they establish much better from seed and potted plants. Some moved as mature plants die because the combination of soil type and sun and drainage and neighbouring plants is not to their liking. The place where they were dug up was very much to their liking, which is why they looked so attractive.

20th April

The sound of wind in the trees was a reminder that winter was still hanging on in the wings, despite the first swallows in the sky.

A thousand feet above sea level, out of the range of traffic noise and sheltered from the biting east wind by trees and tall reeds is a quiet oasis around a pond. It has permanent water, on top of which whirligigg beetles ran round in dizzy circles, honey bees came to drink, and on the bank a wall butterfly was sunning itself. A deer track crossed the ditch near the pond, the sharp pointed imprints deep in the clay hoofprints where the feet had dug into peaty ground.

The pond is usually quiet, but it has its moments. During a recent sunny spell, as the BBC puts it (which always makes me wonder which authority is responsible for getting the incantation right) the pond was a suntrap and the noise of the wind in the trees was joined by a less usual one.

The sound resembled a distant motorcycle. Rrrrk...rrrRRK..... rrrRRK.. but it came from a few feet away in the shallow water of a drainage ditch. A frog's head and pale throat emerged from the pondweed and water, the throat puffing in and out with the sound. The sound resembled a distant motorcycle. Rrrrk...rrrRRK..... rrrRRK.. but it came from a few feet away in a ditch running through the marsh.

Splash. A heavy tandem of male and female frog jumped near him. Instantly the lone frog was after them, swimming desperately to catch up and then attempting to dislodge the male. Pulling, pushing and elbow-butting, he had no success. The tandem continued to travel up the ditch with the attacker in pursuit. Unfortunately at this point the dry rushes under my feet crackled and gave away my presence. Frog and frog pair scuttled down into the mud, not re-emerging while I waited. The sun remained out and a butterfly alighted on the bank. Small midge-like insects swarmed next to the woodland edge. Bees bearing bright yellow pollen sacs on their bodies visited willow catkins, the golden pussy-willows, and came down to the water to drink. Temporarily, it could have been summer.

Talking of summer, I saw one swallow last Monday above Penrith. One swallow hasn't made a summer this year, and it's a struggle to find much of spring. Who first wrote that about one swallow? Aristotle, in the third century BC, according to the Oxford Book of Quotations. And while the book is open, did Shakespeare have anything to say on the subject? Yes, in 'The Winter's Tale,' .."daffodils,

That come before the swallow dares, and take

The winds of March with beauty" ...

4th May

One of the pleasures that I find in watching nature is the way I never know what will turn up next. Sometimes this happens out of the blue, at other times as a result of looking closer into something. Both kinds have come my way this week.

The first was the most comical sight I've seen in the bird world for a long time. A pair of jackdaws landed, as they often do, on a roof in full view of my kitchen window. They turned round to face me and couldn't believe the sight: they both had identical brown false noses. Each beak was crammed, and in fact overcrammed as they dropped bits and shoved them back in, with pieces of brown felt - scavenged from mulching material on the garden.

Another bird find told a different tale, and even had me questioning my sanity. I was high up on a grass hillside above Deepdale when I noticed a pile of white feathers. Alas, Sunday lunch for a peregrine or other hunter. I was picking up a wing feather to find out what sort of bird it had been when I began to see writing on the feather: proper printed writing.

Thoughts flashed through my head - too many hours in front of a hot computer screen and now I was seeing words everywhere. Who would believe a story that started: 'well, I was alone and wandering on a bare hillside away from any paths or people when I saw some white feathers and one of them had writing on it?'. Fortunately the problem solved itself as the writing became clear: a phone number for the pigeon's owner in Workington.

I was struck last year in the hot summer by the great number of mouse holes on steep grassy hillsides, and in the last week or so they have become obvious again. The permanent evidence is little round holes going into grass and bilberry thatch and into the earth under grass and under the edges of rocks. At the moment there is another clue that gives away their locations: grass cutting for bedding. Tufts of grass look as if they've been to the hairdressers, with fresh straight line cuts, and nearby there will be heaps of old cuttings thrown out of the holes.

I rarely walk on grassy fells without seeing the chubby black dor or dung beetle walking across a path. Even with the naked eye the legs show off their fringes and spreading hairs so they almost appear to have ankles and long toes. The body of the beetle is shiny and almost blue-black, but do turn one over: the underside from its head right down to its toes shimmers from electric blue to purple.

***

11th May

Two 'firsts' this week - my first cuckoo of the year and the first greenfly in the garden. I shall keep an eye out for plagues of greenfly on young plant growth, remembering the month of March one dry year some time ago when all the young rose shoots were sucked dry by aphids. This year, however, we may see 'biological control' as there are so many ladybirds around that they may keep the aphids down.

I've been finding ladybirds in many places where they've taken shelter from the winter. The plastic tubes protecting young trees are a favourite with them, as are the buckles of tree ties used to attach young trees to a stake - which incidentally guarantee the death of the tree two to three years after planting if tightened right into the living wood, as can be seen on a recent housing development in Penrith. The doubled-over black plastic buckles usually contain several ladybirds, packed like sardines, together with spiders' eggs, both dry and presumably very warm when the sun shines. Other overwintering places have proved to be the fluffy round seedheads of clematis, especially if the seedhead lodged in the shelter of twigs or branches, loose old bark, and corners of the garden shed.

On the fellsides a relative of the ferns, the club moss *Lycopodium*, is in full 'flower'. This plant, which looks like a small bottle-brush sticking upright out of the ground, is a surviving example of the primitive plant-life which existed hundreds of millions of years ago before any plants had flowers and seeds. Instead, the yellow sacs in the leaf axils produce spores. On a dry day, shaking the plant releases clouds of powdery spores.

Many years ago I was walking in the Czechoslovakian Tatra mountains and scratched my legs badly. The first aid which was produced was a jar of cream-coloured powder, some of which was shaken onto my legs. The powder was the spores of the club moss, pollen-like but much finer than pollen. In fact it's so fine that it will burn, on the same principle as flour will explode from a spark in a mill. I've seen this demonstrated on a large Nepalese clubmoss where shaking and putting a match to the plant made a nice little fireball in the air.

18th May

The morning was calm and ice-cold, although the sun had been up for a couple of hours and had already passed from the early red globe in the mist to yellow brilliance: too bright to look at directly. My footsteps as I walked through a field left a green trail across the silvery-wet grass, between closed dandelion heads, still 'asleep', with no hint of the yellow carpet ready to materialise when all the flowers open.

A footpath running along the bank of the River Eamont from the bridge at Pooley Bridge passes through both woodland and open fields. In the patch of woodland around the start of the path I saw several spring flowers: a few primroses, some patches of wood anemones in full flower and the untidy bushes of wild currant. The leaves of these bushes, if rubbed, smell of black currants.

Patches of leaves looking much like those of the wood anemone proved on closer inspection to bear upright flower stems with small square heads of green flowers. This was the moschatel, also known as 'town hall clock' from the four flowers arranged as sides of square, facing outwards, plus one above these four. Mossy tree stumps at the edge of the wood were covered in a densely-flowering white cress, the spring whitlow grass. This plant is a bit reminiscent in habit, though with bigger petals, of the awful bitter cress of gardens - which even now has ripe seeds ready to throw far and wide should it be pulled up. But this little spring flower doesn't invade gardens and dies down for the rest of the year.

On the river a number of moorhens paddled nervously, flicking their tails. I disturbed a heron before I saw it, and it flew downstream until almost out of sight and onto a shingle bank across the far side. This was not a good choice, as the spot was already occupied by another heron which rose up to send the incomer packing before settling down again.

25th May

This week the scene moves 200 miles north, to Rannoch Moor and Ben Alder Forest in Scotland. These are roadless areas, uninhabited tracts of bog, moor and mountain. They occupy hundreds of square miles between the main north-south routes through Scotland: the A82 via Fort William and the A9 via Aviemore. Incredibly, the mainline railway of the western route, including the reprieved sleeper service from London, diverts from the road into this wilderness, with stations in places that roads do not reach.

When, last Saturday morning, the train pulled out to continue its journey north to Fort William from Corrour, all that remained of civilisation was the rail line disappearing into the distance and the short platform and single building that is all there is at Corrour station. A few birch trees not yet in leaf showed that summer is as far away in Scotland at the end of May as it is further south. As if to make the point quite clear, the east wind suddenly enveloped us in a grey curtain of hail. There was nothing to delay a quick struggle into waterproofs, hats and gloves and setting off into the wind. Our objective was the 'Black Pass' - the Bealach Dubh - leading to the Spey Valley and the Cairngorm mountains.

While the word 'forest' is used for Scottish wilderness areas such as this and the 'Fisherfield Forest', they are bare of trees now. Underfoot for mile after mile is heather and moor-grass, with various sedges and rushes and dwarf shrubs. But where the black peat has eroded into peat hags there are lots of bleached but perfectly-preserved tree stumps, proving that the area was well-forested before the bogs grew. Only where the underlying rock is mineral-rich, the slope steeper and grazing animals excluded are there new trees today.

The Bealach Dubh is a nick in the mountains at merely two thousand feet above sea level. Black may well be the atmosphere normally, but it wasn't on this occasion. After starting in sunshine and showers the rain had set in, and from the beginning of the pass had turned to snow. By the top of the pass the view forward was just sky full of whirling white flakes, more January than May, with wet snow lying on the ground and mountain slopes each side. The snow finally gave out two hours later, just at the point where a wooden board interrupted the path. It bore a notice asking walkers to avoid treading - especially in snow! - On the side of the path where a rare plant - the dwarf birch - grew.

This plant, a small shrub with rounder leaves than the tree birches, was common in England as well as Scotland thousands of years ago. After the glaciers of the Ice Age retreated, and before tree birches, pines and alder colonised the area, dwarf birch was so common that its leaves are often found as fossils. Now however it is scarce, having been eliminated by both dense woodland and by sodden peat.in the former forests and disliking pure peat to grow in. This particular patch seems to be doing well despite walkers and deer. Its Ice Age links certainly fitted the day's conditions.

1st June

The location remains central Scotland this week, below a freshly-snowclad Ben Alder. After the snow, down in the valley, the rain came down in torrents. Fortunately by then we were inside the four walls of a bothy to watch its progress through the long daylight hours of evening. A couple of cyclists turned up who hadn't been so fortunate: they were as wet as if they'd walked through the nearby lake.

After the rain, the next morning, it was a damp day with low cloud. Still not a midge in sight, nor any other flies. A cuckoo was calling, and oyster-catchers flew screaming over a nearby riverbed. The damp earth of the path told the tale of visitors during the night. Deep wedge-shaped deer prints passed the house and continued into muddy ditches and over the pathside grass, churning up the peat as badly as any party of walkers.

As we continued our route to Loch Ericht, we turned a corner and found ourselves opposite a group of five deer at the edge of a pine wood. And then twenty or so more, and then a herd of a hundred at least, occupying our side of the hill up to the skyline. They saw us, continued grazing, while a female and her year-old adolescent took refuge behind the trees. Slowly the rest moved a little further away from us. In the poor light the most noticeable part of them, giving away the position of half-hidden animals, were the pale patches on the rump. I was reminded of other white flashes as animals and birds retreat: moorhen flick up white ovals on their tails, and hares and rabbits show off white, not camouflaged, tufts.

On every damp, uncultivated field lapwings wheeled around, reminding us to keep off the grass, where their just-hatched chicks could be trodden on by accident. By scanning the area very carefully from outside, knowing that the chicks had to be there somewhere, I picked out a group of four speckled young. As the adults yelled at them and us, three of the four chicks ran to a tuft of rushes and became still and invisible. Only young Fred, or perhaps it was Freda, stayed out in the open exploring a fascinating mole-hill. I moved on, hoping the chick would be rounded up by its parents before one of the marauding crows grabbed it.

15th June

Back in Cumbria, the River Eden was so still in the evening that the surface of the water across the other side resembled dark green glass, on which black and white tufted ducks had been added for artistic effect. Tree trunks and greenery of the opposite bank were mirrored almost perfectly, and as I gazed into the water a slate-grey reflection passed clearly across the scene and came to rest in the reflected leaves. Looking from the mirror to the real world found the heron perched in full view on top of a tree.

Around the next corner is one of those shallow, pebbly cascades where the water runs noisily down to the next calm section. As it came into view, so did a line, in single file, of wild geese. The line, of about 40 adults and young, was descending the mini-rapids towards a large group idling in the middle of the river. As they neared the end of the rough water, most ran into difficulty, perhaps touching the stony bottom as they paddled, and they flapped and half-flew to the group in the calm stretch below.

Along the path, where sunlight reached the ground, spring flowers produced a pink, white and blue colour scheme. I saw a patch of pure white forget-me-not flowers amongst the vivid blue, and the dame's violet as usual in all shades between white, pink and purple.

All at once the gentle noise of the river, the humming of bees on a holly tree in flower, the occasional cry of oyster-catchers and squawk of moorhen was interrupted by a great crowd of rooks and crows. They flew in a large flock, 'cawing' at the tops of their voices. I was looking for the cause when a sharp form dashed into the flock, one wing vertical and as menacing as a shark's fin. The battle moved behind the hilltop, and I don't know who won. But there was noise for a long time.

Returning along the same track, I travelled in hope of seeing new things: perhaps the face behind the rustlings in the undergrowth as a small animal ran along and froze when I tried to see it. I brushed through many strands of gossamer across the path, so spiders at least had been busy. But, as so often, what turned up was totally unexpected. I had forgotten to stop and listen to the holly-tree to see if it still hummed, but I suspect that it didn't. For on a dead tree was a swarm of bees, a mass of bees at least a foot in diameter, with still more arriving.

22nd June

I find myself suffering from empty nest syndrome. Literally. For the bluetit brood in the nest box flew away yesterday, and I miss their chatter. And I miss the parents' day-long labours bringing green caterpillars every couple of minutes, from far and wide. A successful meals on wings service.

In a local woodland I spotted a trail of ants. Interested to see if I could follow it back to the nest, I traced first the far point where the ants spread out, up tree trunks and over the leaf litter. Half a dozen in the trail were dragging small green caterpillars - the sort that hang down from oak trees on a thread - over tree roots, banks and all obstacles. Some had two or more individuals helping with the task, and I saw a second ant come to the aid of a single carrier when it was getting nowhere on a complex of tree roots. I overtook the procession and paced out the length of the trail: fifty yards to the nest, where the caterpillars were thrust down holes. Other ants were bringing the fragments of dried leaf, catkin and twig that makes up the compost-heap of the nest.

29th June

Here be dragons. Well, OK, not actual dragons breathing fire but nevertheless scaly creatures which were around during the time of the dinosaurs and are still around. They are definitely carnivorous and perpetually hungry. The large reptile-like eyes never miss a potential meal, the muscular tail flicks them along to jump on the unsuspecting prey, and the jaws can chomp up live fish.

These fearsome creatures are the larvae of dragonflies. For a year or two the brown young live under water in ponds and lakes among weeds and mud. Then, one summer day, they crawl up and out of the water, the skin splits, and out comes the adult dragonfly with shimmering wings. If ever there were a case of a frog turning into a prince it is this transformation.

I was lucky enough to be looking at a pond on a very hot afternoon last week when a head appeared alongside a thick spearwort stem. Two legs and then all six legs - for this is an insect - appeared and pulled the body up the stem. The huge protruding eyes were scale-covered and shut. The larva pulled up a bit, rested, and repeated this until it was almost out of the water - and then fell off. The tail lashed, it started again. And eventually made it. The new adult emerged from a split in the back of the skin, unfolded, dried out and flew away leaving the old skin behind.

* * *

While walking beyond Watendlath I saw a neat rounded tree on the fellside, exactly half of which was covered in apple blossom. Inspection showed that the other side of the tree was a rowan, and the two trees, crab apple and rowan were growing side by side on one trunk. I recall having seen less tidy examples of rowans mixed up in other trees, but never so clearly.

'Oh yes', said someone I recounted this to, 'that's a flying rowan. They're supposed to have magic powers'. No doubt. Perhaps I'll encounter them when I return for a closer look, and try to satisfy my curiosity about how the rowan does this trick.

6th July

Arctic-alpine usually have compact growth with a lot of flower in proportion to leafy stem. They are treasured for rock gardens. In the wild, they come from high mountains and the far north, either above or beyond the treeline. We are lucky enough to have a tiny selection in the Pennines and Lakeland, including arguably the most beautiful of all, the spring gentian. Found nowhere else in England, it dots the pastures of Teesdale with vivid blue while the bird's eye primrose nearby in an enclosure to keep out the sheep creates a sheet of pink.

During the ice age these plants and others like the cushion plant *Silene acaulis* and the purple mountain saxifrage were common as weeds in England. There were thousands of them all over what is now London. Growing with them, as we know from abundant fossil seeds, were 'real' weeds like chickweed and dandelions. What a pity it is that the gentians and saxifrages were too fussy to join them in taking up the lifestyle of a weed in our fields and gardens. Or perhaps if they had, we wouldn't notice their beauty. If dandelions were only known from one patch of plants on the top of a mountain, would we think them beautiful?

13th July

Sunrise comes late to pastures and lakes in the shadow of mountains. Thus it was that a fortnight ago I stood at the edge of a lake as the first rays of direct light arrived. I was expecting the reflections of orange fluffy clouds and green fellsides to become clearer, but instead the mirror disappeared and the water became pitted and rippled as if under a rain shower. A cloud of insects emerged and then the water smoothed over again.

Other creatures clearly were newly emerged. A shiny new and very elegant golden-ringed dragonfly was quite happy to sit on my hand as I explored the area. He was three inches long, black with yellow bands on the body. Yes, he was a 'he', as male and female dragonflies can be told apart by the differently-shaped tails. The black and yellow was quite striking: was he, I wondered, getting benefit from imitating a wasp with this colouring? In the state that I found him he would have been a nice meal for a predator.

Along the heather-covered slope were caterpillars of the northern oak eggar moth, big orangey-brown bristly creatures. I've often had to step aside for these when walking on moorland in the summer. But I'd never seen the moths, and here were newly-emerged adults clinging to plant stems while the wings vibrated. The bodies were fat, furry, and like the wings an ochre to sand colour. The females are famous for attracting males from a long way out of sight by emitting a very effective scent known as a pheromone. Apparently the male can smell it a mile away and is led up the scent path right to the originator.

That is, of course, if the new moths survive their first hours. Just past the new arrivals the brown peat of the path was decorated with groups of neatly-severed yellow wings. Of the fat bodies there was not a scrap left.

Talking of bodies becoming somebody's lunch, I revisited the top of the hill where earlier this year I had found a pile of racing pigeon feathers. Looking for somewhere for a rest stop that would be out of the wind, I made my way into a deeply-cut ravine below a waterfall where there was a terrace big enough to accommodate a rucksac and myself. The ground was carpeted with alpine lady's mantle, quite a common plant on the Lake District fells, and at my selected spot this carried a heap of white feathers. Just like the time before, there was no body. Unlike the time before, however, there was no phone number on any of the remaining wing feathers.

20th July

Armathwaite in the early morning was sitting in a pool of mist, while the river surface steamed as the relatively warm water passed through this colder air. The water level is low again, exposing shelves of solid rock, and by taking one of the well-defined deer and badger paths down the steep bank, I was able to walk into the centre of the river to take photographs.

The first object of interest was an unintentional nest-box for ducks. A section of old iron machinery sticks out of the water and has provided a solid frame for a nest of grass and reeds. Whether this particular nest has been deserted I don't know, but although it contained an egg there was no bird nearby. The second was the overhanging tree branches still bearing tufts of flood debris - quite a way above my head. It was strange to imagine that the quiet sunlit rock that I was standing on had been, and no doubt will be again one day, ten feet under surging flood water.

The jungle of plants on the bank included a few spots of colour. Pink and gold martagon lilies are at their best just now, and pale bellflowers are just coming out. The Himalayan balsam is doing poorly so far, with only a few flowers to be seen. But some plants are very vigorous, including a specimen of marsh thistle which is the biggest I have ever seen, somewhere around seven feet high.

Huge leaves of butterbur were massed between the road and the river. As big as an umbrella, and a bit like outsize colts-foot leaves, the butterbur leaves only grow up after the early spring flowers have finished. Next to them were wild rasp-berry plants, the fruits a long way away from ripe. And, as I found to my cost when I returned to the road through the middle of the jungle, it was full of nettles.

Reaching the road I disturbed two hares which ran away down the road, and a mouse rustling in the leaves, which dashed into a hole at the bottom of the wall. I waited. A few minutes later the mouse appeared higher up in the wall and looked out - and saw me and vanished again. I put a few crumbs of cake at this hole in the wall. At last there was a flicker of movement, and a face appeared. But if wasn't the mouse. It was a new character, a shrew. It sniffed the cake, obviously was not taken with it, and went away. I sat for a long time but the mouse never reappeared.

27th July

I was heading towards home from Appleby at half past ten in the evening, or perhaps I should say 'at night', for a month after the longest day the road required headlights and the high hedges and trees were solid black against the sky. Yet the surrounding countryside could still be seen per-fectly clearly due to a bright half-moon and the pale blue sky to the north.

The air between the hedges along this quiet road was so full of insects - beetles, moths, flies and midges - that it was like driving through thin soup. Several bats flew around in this abundant and varied menu.

The road climbed to the crest of a small hill, and in the mid-dle of the road at the top, beautifully silhouetted against the sky, was a hare. It ran down the road in front of me until I stopped, and it stopped - in the middle of the road. A car came in the opposite direction and the animal panicked as it was trapped between two sets of lights, but eventually it found the edge of the road. Four minutes later I came across a second hare emerging from a front garden.

* * *

Earlier in the week I visited Lanty's tarn at Glenridding in the evening. A clear stream was running into the shallow tarn, which although lower than usual still contained plenty of water and shoals of small fish. Originally a natural pond, belonging to one Lancelot Dobson, it now has a dam at the end and an ice house nearby can still be seen.

As I walked between the winter 'tide-line' and the water, on ground described as 'squidge' by one young walker, I realised that there were creatures moving underfoot, the size of beetles or spiders. I looked down and then hastily removed myself to drier land to avoid treading on them. What was moving was a vast number of young toads and froglets leaving the tarn for the land.

The two components of this migration army were easily distinguished. The young frogs were perfect miniatures of the adult, coloured light yellow with brown patches, and their long legs unfolded as they jumped. The toads, blackish and camouflaged wonderfully well within the pits of sheep footprints in the peaty soil, could only crawl their way along.

The tadpoles in my pond are still tadpoles: I wonder if they, coming from frogspawn laid later than average, in an exposed situation, are still late compared with the average or if Lanty's tarn with its belts of sheltering trees around is particularly forward.

3rd August

During the dry weather I started putting apple cores on the bird table, where the blackbirds quickly removed the remaining flesh. As this had been a success, I did the same with nectarine stones with fruit on - and found them cleaned up immediately. I've discovered what blackbirds really like! My only worry is that having given them a taste for fruit they'll help themselves to fruit on the trees with the same enthusiasm.

The bedraggled male blackbird who looked as if he had been pulled through a hedge backwards is no longer around, but one without a tail has taken over the area immediately around the house. Several of this year's young birds are now independent and are foraging along the base of walls and flower borders, scattering leaves and moss onto the lawn. Groups of old and young frequent the pond, where they enjoy a wash and brush-up together with starlings and sparrows.

There hasn't been a day recently without the sight and sound of goldfinches. I've come across them on quiet roadside verges, in fields, in towns and in gardens, balancing on the tips of wild plants like sorrel, thistle and groundsel to eat the seeds. They twitter with a high-pitched note as they fly, but when they perch on wires and sing the song has, to me, a liquid quality as if emerging from underwater in a clear river.

While out gathering gooseberries during the week I had the company of an even smaller bird than the goldfinch: a little warbler. Light brown above and white beneath, it was so light that it perched on the tips of branches without bending them. It kept up an incessant two-note 'too-wit', a sound I've heard before in hedgerows this summer but never been sure that it belonged to anything other than a chaffinch.

This bird I believe was a willow warbler; certainly it was one of the pair of species including the chiff-chaff and the willow warbler which are almost identical in appearance.

Wasps' nests are something I associate with the loft or the inside of a shed or in the the corner of the compost heap, although last year I encountered one underground in almost pure sand. The nests are made of grey paper-like material, hardening like papier maché, produced from fresh wood shavings. I often hear wasps chewing, taking off minute strips of wood from my garden shed and trellis, leaving a pattern of parallel lines. They are also frequent visitors to the pond, alighting on pondweed leaves to drink or maybe to gather water for their paper material.

I was fascinated last weekend to be shown a wasps' nest out in the open on a branch of an apple tree. It was the first time I'd been able to stand in the sunshine and watch a nest being built. Relating this to a friend, I was told of another nest in the area out in the open, started and grown to full size in a currant bush. Is this a new trend, I wonder?

10th August

A photographer that I once knew carried around with him some old and bleached sheep bones. Then when he needed a foreground for a landscape photograph, out came the bones and instantly an artistic composition was achieved. It also looked perfectly natural - at least for the first dozen appearances of the bones.

I was reminded of his compositions when I stood at the side of the River Lowther near Askham. The scene could have passed for a painting of rural England - but in the style of a picture composed in a studio for maximum emotional effect. The problem was that there were just too many appealing elements. No-one would have believed that all the animals and birds were actually there rather than added from a box of countryside clip art.

The background was a sunlit hillside with cows grazing and a trio of buzzards soaring high in the sky. From this the river wound into the foreground, where rabbits stood on the grazed turf with erect ears and bright brown eyes, ready to dash down a burrow at any disturbance. The near water's edge was a mass of yellow mimulus and blue forget-me-nots, with taller yellow loosestrife, aromatic mint and woundwort. The far bank plunged straight down to the water, with masses of lilac bellflowers interrupting the solid green vegetation. Their colour was reflected in the water and then repeated in the purple of a heron flapping slowly by.

On the open water, perfectly arranged artistically, was a lone swan, a family of goosanders and a group of mallard. Grey wagtails flitted over the stones and a moorhen squawked as it race-walked to its family in the reeds. Five Canada geese on the bank got up and moved onto the water and floated downstream toward the swan, which raised its wings and swam at them.

The geese split into two groups, a group of three which retreated and a pair which circled wide to the river edge, around the swan and continued downstream. This was the type of problem I imagine a sheepdog would enjoy, but would the swan manage the two groups? The swan didn't noticeably move a muscle, but I noticed that the two geese had started grunting softly, and then they turned round and joined the other group in retreat from the swan.

17th August

Latin names of plants, more than those of animals, give rise to many moans and groans. The vocabulary is a mixture of Greek and Latin with a lot of personal and geographical names thrown in, and is a lot to absorb. The names are doing two incompatible jobs at once, the first being to give the plant a name as a label so that everyone knows exactly which plant is being referred to, in England and Equador and East Timor. Secondly, the names are points in the classification system.

So if we take the corn marigold that is blooming on the strip of land by Langwathby bridge, its Latin name is *Chrysanthemum*. However, botanists have decided that it and the cut flowers we buy called chrysanthemums belong to different categories - different genera. So which has to change its name?

There is a set of internationally-agreed rules for naming plants which says roughly that the first name given to a plant post-1753 must be used. Rummaging around in old books has often stirred up problems, but it is the source of a new name when one is required.

It was discovered that our corn marigold claimed the earliest association with the name Chrysanthemum, so the cultivated one had to change. In this way just when you and I and the world and the E.C. all knew that those long-lasting flowers bought in florists' shops are called Chrysanthemum - both in Latin and in English - they changed to *Dendranthema*. Confusion all round! At one point it got so bad that I remember experts using the label "Florists' 'mum" to refer to these flowers.

24th August

What sort of fruits do blackthorn bushes produce? Sloes of course. So when someone with sharp eyes told me that some had produced long pods, I was puzzled to say the least.

I found the bushes in question, each of which indeed had grown brown woody pods arising in the position of fruits in addition to normal sloes. Because the pods had started as fruits and then grown into an alien shape and colour, I suspected that they were galls and that I would find a grub inside, as one does with oak apples and many other lumps and bumps on plants. But these pods were hollow and empty.

Years ago - I notice the price on the jacket is '25 shillings' - I bought myself the 'Pocket Encyclopaedia' of plant galls, so at this point I got it off the shelf and looked up blackthorn in the index. Bingo. A picture of the pods. No wonder they seemed quite empty inside: they are empty, and have nothing to do with any insect. Instead, this infection is a fungus called 'bladder bullace fungus', related to the peach leafcurl, and it is on the outside only of the pod it induces.

This week has seen two butterfly species return which have been very rare since the cold spring, the peacock and the red admiral. The best place to look for them is buddleia bushes, where they've joined the huge numbers of painted ladies so that each branch of flowers often has three or four butterflies prodding for nectar. As well as butterflies these bushes are frequented by bees and at the moment an occasional silver-Y moth. These grey-brown, perpetually-vibrating moths often feed on the wing, but on the buddleia they come may to rest and allow the silver mark on the wing to be seen. Just like the butterflies, they push their long tongue down the middle of a flower to the nectar. But unlike butterflies they are keen on unscented everlasting pea flowers, where they cheat by probing down the back petals of the flower and not through the centre.

31st August

Mushrooms and toadstools are becoming much more common as the season slips into autumn. Woodland floors are happy hunting grounds for the amazing variety of coloured toadstools, while dead and even living trees carry forms from dry 'brackets' to the soft pinky-brown ear-shaped cups on elder branches. Going on half a day's fungus-hunting, known as a 'fungus foray', with a local expert is something I've always found fun and interesting, and I hope to catch one of the forays run by the National Park or the East Cumbria Countryside Project this year.

For the past month or so one particular fungus has been smelled but not seen along woodland walks. Once encountered the smell is always recognisable, but hard to describe. Sweetish and stinky combined, perhaps. Tracking down the fungus responsible is not too difficult, if the concentration of smell is followed and then a search instigated under bracken or saplings for the culprit. Occasionally it is in plain view in the open, and recently the riverside footpath at Armathwaite had dozens on the leaf-mould at intervals along the edge of the path.

The culprit is of course the aptly-named stinkhorn, an extraordinary form of toadstool. The shape gives it its Latin name - *Phallus impudicus*. Usually seen past its pristine state, on a cool day such as the one when I saw so many at Armathwaite it is possible to see the white stalks erect and the cap fully covered with a wet brown coating of spores. In a few hours the brown has all been removed by flies to disperse the spores to new localities.

Having found a group of stinkhorns, it's worth searching around their bases for the 'eggs' from which they emerge. The egg is a mushroom-coloured sphere a couple of inches across attached to underground root-like fibres. Cutting one in half vertically shows a cross section of the stalk and cap waiting to emerge in one or a few days' time. The eggs can be moved - try taking one home to the garden and watching it emerge: but be ready to for complaints from family and neighbours!

7th September

When I moved house and acquired an extent of stones, thistles and ragworts called a garden, my first project was to dig a pond. Lakes and ponds have always drawn me to them, for the beauty of still water and water-plants and for the number of creatures in and around a wet area. So now I could create one to watch every day.

The digging itself was interesting, showing the soil to be largely sand with soft sandstone just under the surface. There were many exceedingly heavy blueish boulders, rounded and broken, which must have been brought here by glaciers as well as broken pottery and clay pipe stems. White roots of thistles were encountered all the way down to more than three feet, rooted in solid sandstone - perhaps the thistles which keep on appearing are from these original roots rather than newly-seeded.

The pond, now two years old, has given immense interest from the first day. Some creatures such as dragonflies, damselflies and beetles just arrived. I brought in some frogspawn and have one two-year-old frog from this resident in the pond, and others under the compost heap and elswhere. I was given some common newts this year, which produced young. I sowed seed of water forget-me-not, loosestrifes and irises on the banks and they have thrived and spread. But I made a mistake in importing a forkful of plants cleared out from a mature lake.

My aim was to add a variety of species mimicking a mature pond, the weeds and small creatures providing interest in their own right and providing shelter and food for the larger inhabitants. Alas, it has turned into a paradise for carnivores. Dragonfly larvae and the aquatic bug known from its pair of oar-like extended leg as the water boatman are the worst. The latter hangs around, upside-down in the water and waits for potential meals to appear. A vicious predator, it is the pond's equivalent of Tyranosaurus rex.

During the summer wasps often come to the pond for water, alighting on pond-weed leaves. One day I saw the body of one overhang the leaf, and two water boatmen immediately rushed at it. There was a fierce battle leaving all three dead. Then this week I spotted the silver flash from the back of a water boatman burying itself in the mud. Sticking up from the place where it had disappeared was a tail - horribly recognisable as that of a newt. I scooped up the tail and surrounding mud in a net and discovered a dead newt in the jaws of the predator. That's nature. But it's my pond, and I like newts, so action will follow.

14th September

"It's a long, long while

From May to December;

And the days grow short

When you reach September"

Maxwell Anderson, 1938.

It hardly seems a long time since last winter, but the outdoor scene tells us that the flowering season is winding down. Along roadsides and riversides plants are fruiting and seeding; millions of seeds are being shed onto the ground to compete with each other next year. And to spread to new places by riverside floods, by wind and even on the socks of walkers. Very obvious now are the sweet cicely's heads of black seeds, poppies' pepper-pots, and the extra-large dandelion-like heads of goat's beard.

There are few roadsides now without willowherb releasing masses of silky parachutes to drift through the air. Willowherbs are called willowherbs because they imitate the fluffy down on willow seeds. Looking back to spring and the pussy-willows of the hedgerows, some trees bear gold flowers and some silvery-green. These are the male and the female flowers, borne on separate male and female trees. It is the female trees only which bear seed and let them loose attached to silky tufts.

While willow trees flower and fruit early in the year there is one species which is only now spreading its fluff around. I came across it on a mountain walk across Crag Hill in the northwestern Lake District. I noticed little masses of fluff on the ground around the summit. I didn't think twice about this debris until I came to an area of solid willows and saw the fluff emerging from ripe catkins amongst the leaves.

Now before my readers jump up and down saying there aren't any trees on these summits, I haven't actually said willow 'tree'. I do like to think of this willow as a minute tree, but the plant in question is only an inch high and a walking boot covers many individuals. Its name is the 'least willow', in Latin *Salix herbacea*. It is quite common on the summits of the northern fells where the climate is severe, the ground broken up by freezing and thawing and no extensive grass sward can survive. Looking a bit like a grazed bilberry, the flowers and fruits at ground level will readily distinguish it. It appears not to suffer from being walked over unseen by many a vibram sole.

A tree which doesn't look happy at the end of summer is the sycamore. Several can be seen with brown, dead leaves, perhaps due to continued shortage of rain. And perhaps the tar-spot fungus, which causes black spots on the leaves, has contributes to the stress.

21st September

It was the movement of leaves in the crown of a hazel tree which gave away its presence. There was no wind at all in the valley last Sunday morning , and the surface of Ullswater was like glass. Trees stood still and perfectly-reflected in the water. So there was something in that tree, and my hopes rose as the movement continued without a large bird emerging. Then the movement shifted and a very gingery-red squirrel ran down the trunk of the nut tree.

My object for the day was to check the route and timing for a walk up the fells, so I left the Squirrel Nutkin to his breakfast and walked through light woodland onto the bare sheep pastures. The trees hadn't yet turned colour in the way of the leaves getting autumn tints, but the ash trees were strikingly yellow-green from the unusually large bunches of 'keys'. Hawthorns which had been so smothered in white flowers in the early summer look as if they'll be putting on another show in a week or two, when the berries turn red.

The next stage of the walk had few flowers, the colour in the valley coming from sedges and rushes turning red or gold, and bogs with multi-coloured mosses. Most of the landscape was the coarse *nardus* grass that sheep leave alone. But almost at the top, on the crags above my path, the natural vegetation was once again woodland - though fragmented onto individual precipices where seedlings had managed to grow up undisturbed.

Grey-green juniper spread over rocks as attractively as in a rock garden - indeed this is the original from which we try to design our miniature imitations! Birch and rowan trees were thriving with roots twisting and spreading over and under scree and cracks in the rock wall. Holly always surprises me by its appearance high up ravines and cliffs in the mountains, especially as male and female trees must be present, and fit enough to flower, for the females to produce berries and young trees to keep establishing themselves. The other surprise to me with the holly is the softness of the new leaves - not prickly at all as yet. No wonder animals love browsing them.

28th September

I have been re-reading Oliver Rackham's 'The History of the Countryside', especially in relation to hedges. My interest is not unrelated to recent hours spent brambling, getting sharply acquainted with a number of examples. One in particular had a stretch not only producing huge blackberries but was a riot of colour, scarlet rosehips mingling with blue sloes amongst reddening hawthorn fruits.

Musing on this - and possession of a container with some brambles is a perfect prop for standing around in the countryside doing nothing very much - I recalled that the number of species in a hedge has been found to be proportional to its age. This made sense where I was: on an old green track outside Skirwith. The trackway was hedged both sides, and the hedges looked undisturbed for a long time. Blackthorn, hawthorn, various roses, gooseberry, crab apple, ash, oak, hazel, aspen and elm were the main ingredients, with several large trees of ash, oak and elm.

Thorny plants, as I'd discovered first-hand, are well represented. This ties in with a hedge being a boundary. But what of the tall trees? I read that historically hedges were a source of serious timber, the emergent trees being the right shape for roof timbers and for shipbuilding. Firewood was collected from the base, and the gooseberry and other fruit bushes encouraged. So the hedge I was looking at was not just a boundary but also was a linear wood with a capital value, supplying products, and at the same time was a garden extension with fruit.

Rackham gives several examples of people convicted of stealing wood or live bushes from a hedgerow, and quotes an Essex edict in 1567:

"Any persons breaking any hedge or stealing any wood be put next Sunday or holyday in the stocks for 2 hours at the least, and the wood be placed before them, signifying the cause of the punishment".

Driving back to Langwathby, I kept half an eye on the hedges. There was a very different look to these: almost pure hawthorn. I'm not knocking these, as they provide shelter and food for wild life. But now I've become aware of the treasures we have in the colourful and fruitful mixed hedges, this is the time of year to discover them.

One of the 'treasures' I put in my pocket at the weekend was an acorn fallen from the majestic oak tree at the entrance to Nunnery Walks. The glossy brown acorn was still attached in its cup, which was woolly and fringed with green mossy scales, showing that the tree is a Turkey oak, a planted species originating in southern Europe and indeed Turkey. It makes, as at Nunnery, a large tree in a short time, but its timber is weak compared with that of our native oaks.

With my mind still on edibles in the hedgerows, I wondered if acorns of any species of oak are worthwhile food for human consumption. I've tried ordinary acorns, which are boring. The first answer I got was interesting: the Turkey oak acorn is reputed to be the worst-tasting, most bitter kind. But *Quercus robur*, one of our two native oak species, is high up the league table for taste, and like many oaks of America, can be ground into a bread flour and has been recorded from historical and prehistorical sources. Bitter if untreated, on account of the tannins which pervade all parts of the oak, the flour becomes sweet if washed in boiling water before cooking mixing into bread or cakes.

Fungus-hunting will probably be better this weekend than last, as the dry weather still had a hold on woodland floors. One toadstool however is flourishing on lawns and road-sides: the 'lawyer's wig' or shaggy ink-cap. And yes, it's edi-ble. But unlike mushrooms you can't collect it and store it for another day. From being a beautiful firm white cylinder the base soon starts to disappear in a wet black mess and this moves upwards to engulf the whole cap. And there goes your gourmet meal - a puddle of ink at the bottom of the fridge.

Do be sure you've got the right kind of ink-cap. While many related ones are harmless, the first cousin to the lawyer's wig is a woodland and field ink-cap, more of a standard toadstool in shape and dirtier-coloured, which is the source of antabuse. This is the drug which reacts rather badly with alcohol, and has been used medically for this purpose.

5th October

I promise that I will move off the subject of fruit in the hedgerows next time. But this week I am still under the influence of the bright reds and purples that are such a feature of our countryside hedges this month. Hawthorn trees are becoming redder by the day, looking as if they've had a punk hairstyle as the green crown is enveloped in a deep red cover of berries. Although the brambles are on their way out, there is still fruit to pick, and the pleasure of exploring the natural variation in size and flavour from one plant to another.

Confession time again. I thought a damson was a damson and that was all there was to it. Thinking of getting myself a tree some time, I had in mind just to order a damson tree from a nursery. That was before I came across the Westmorland Damson Association. I learnt that there is a very special damson variety with a wonderful flavour and grown particularly in the Lyth Valley, called the Westmorland Damson. Unfortunately the orchards are in decline and the great snowy displays of blossom in spring are no longer a tourist sight. The WDA exists to reverse the decline and to spread awareness of the damson. People are encouraged to grow the tree, but the only way to get a tree is to propagate by vegetative shoots. The flowers will accept pollen from all sorts of related plums and the seeds therefore don't breed true.

A wild relation of the damson is the bullace. It has round fruits, sloe-like but plain acid rather than the sloe's mouth-drying effect. I've been shown dark purple bullaces, green-purple ones and seen pictures of greengage-coloured ones. Reference books fail to agree at all on whether its a species or subspecies or hybrid of the domestic plum. The best answer seems to be that, like apples, all these plum-like plants are promiscuous, but distinct varieties settle out locally or where propagated widely by growers. However, whatever its parentage, it can be used in cooking just like damsons and plums.

On the subject of preserving our heritage of local fruit tree varieties, the English apple has had a bad time recently and has largely been dropped by selectors for the English supermarket chains. Local Cumbrian apples may not be suitable to play in this league, but include some fine flavours and the ability to grow in a cooler climate.

To identify the varieties in Cumbria, and stop old varieties becoming extinct, the Cumbria Apple Forum came into being. Its mission is to find out which lesser-known, older apples are growing in Cumbria, to restore run-down orchards and save the old apples from extinction. It is holding an afternoon of events to celebrate the British apple, with emphasis on local apples, at Acorn Bank, near Temple Sowerby, on Sunday October 20 from 2pm. Old apple varieties can be identified, the orchard visited, and there will be entertainments.

19th October

Two days after the rain stopped the fells were still running with water. The lines of pondweed, normally marking damp tracks through springy moss and grass, were now fed with so much water that they had become deep channels filled with crystal-clear water. The soft peat and moss had been cleared out by the force of running water to produce pools several feet deep - a real trap for the unwary. The classic walkers' comment 'there might be a dead sheep at the top of that clear stream you're drinking' was unfortunately all too true, with one of the victims still in a standing position underwater, gently mummifying in the pool at the top of the network of streams.

A nicer find was masses of bladderwort in the streams. This is an uncommon species of water plant, looking like a pale asparagus fern floating in the current. The hair-like leaves are interspersed with numerous little bladders easily visible to the naked eye. The bladders work on the same principle as a lobster pot, allowing little creatures to swim in but not out, and the plant proceeds to digest them.

Its flowers arise on stalks emerging into the air, though they are rarely found. The flowers are perfectly 'normal', asymmetric with a spur and two-lipped petals. This gives away its relationships, for apart being yellow and not purple in colour, the flower is just like that of the butterwort. This latter is another of our three moorland plants which supplement their diet with catching and digesting small animals. The third of these, sundew, is common on acidic bogs.

Moving off the flat boggy areas onto grass slopes, I came across a cluster of scarlet fly agaric toadstools standing out against the yellowing bracken and fallen birch leaves. Not one was perfect, but each cap had a white hole where a slug had eaten through the red skin. In contrast, smaller pink toadstools in the same locality were untouched. These pink ones were a kind of *lactarius*, a toadstool characterised by white milky sap. If touched to the tongue the milk in some of our *lactarius* species is hotter than a chilli pepper.

26th October

Halloween marks the letting go of leaves from the trees and strong sunshine and the positive growth of summer. From ancient times it has been a festival to mark the gateway into the dark and cold winter season, attended by the black image of the witch. Just now this seems a long way away. We are enjoying summer temperatures and I have seen a fresh wild rose in flower this week, among the scarlet hips of the hedgerow. It seems unbelievable that any time now we will be plunged into frost and snow.

Looking back at my Notes for this time last year, I see a very similar picture. Apart from the devastating frost in September we had the same southerly winds right through to November. Shrubs flowered and butterflies persisted in the garden and the wild. Like this year, autumn colours on the trees came in late and patchily.

I walked up the road between town and countryside. A flock of goldfinches rose up ahead of me, twittering, and moved on to the next patch of thistles and docks. Both plants have nice solid seeds to eat, thought the thistle tops its seeds with a fluffy parachute. I have not been close enough to see how birds deal with the fluff but, having watched other finches deal with sunflower seeds - pick up, split the husk, spit out, and swallow the seed - I am sure there is a technique for thistles.

Under the hedges there are some small foxgloves in flower and masses of foxglove plants. They are biennial, which means that last year's years seeds produced these plants, which will flower next year. Also in the sprawl of uncut vegetation in the verge, where a month ago the goosegrass covered everything in a sticky mat, two vetches are in flower. The bush vetch has a few purple flowers turning a strange watered-ink blue on fading while the pretty tufted vetch has deep blue flowerspikes.

My favourite flower of the moment for elegance is the harebell. I particularly like the combination of harebell flowers and red stonework of the bridges over the River Eden. The sun shining through the translucent blue of the petals is just one element of my personal fondness for autumn.

2nd November

Mountain streams last Sunday tumbled down their rocky courses as white as snow, the sun showing up droplets scattered high above the cascades. As they flowed down they gathered still more water from dripping moss. It looked like an endless row of taps not quite turned off. I demonstrated the Sphagnum sponge effect: pick up a handful of this moss, hold it away from you and squeeze. A stream of water runs out.

It's just as well that sponge and peat cover the hills: I tried to imagine what it would be like if nothing delayed the water and the streams took in a hundred times as much. As well as the water there would be rocks moved around and thrown out at bends and the bottom of slopes. Once I walked by the river Tees in flood, and the sound of huge boulders on the river bed moving against each other with unearthly groans is something I've never forgotten.

The rowan tree, or mountain ash, grows in ravines above mountain streams as well as in more hospitable places. This year I have become intrigued by its habit of growing on other trees, no doubt arriving as a seed via birds. Plenty of mature trees have a coating of moss and ferns and enough resulting soil to accommodate the odd squatter, and such things as rose-bay willow herb and small elders are often found on old trees. But I haven't found a really big "squatter" tree of the other species with bird-carried fruits, or any other type for that matter.

Half way between Watendlath and Dock Tarn a nice round tree can be seen against a wall in the adjacent field. But what tree is it? Exactly half, on the left, is a crab apple and half, on the right, a rowan. Suspecting that the rowan might really be growing in the ground with a trunk closely pressed to that of the apple, I had a close look. No. The thick trunk started up the apple trunk, and was forcing the apple bark to split as it thickened. Has the rowan forced its way down to the soil inside the apple trunk? I don't know.

The rowan has magic powers ascribed to it. It traditionally wards off witches, evil and bad luck, as a tree planted by the house and as twigs carried both everyday and as part of the Scots' clan dress. Scandinavia has the same superstition, the plant being associated with the god Thor. Why the rowan? Perhaps because of the abundant red berries and striking appearance in fruit; perhaps because it is common in the playground of the old gods: the mountains. Could it also have anything to do with the magic feat of growing up on another tree?

9th November

I had forgotten the peculiarly autumn smell of walking through damp fallen leaves, but recognised it at once as I swished my way along the pavement this week. Similarly the aroma of curry lurking around oak trees brings back memories of autumn walks. For years I believed the smell to come from the oak tree itself, but one day on a Fungus Foray I was shown the little toadstool on the ground which is the real culprit.

* * *

New National Nature Reserves in Cumbria have been announced. One is at Cliburn Moss, along the road past Wetheriggs Pottery to the south of Whinfell Forest. The Moss is what is called a 'raised bog', an area of mosses and bog plants growing upwards complete with their own water table, so that the bog becomes convex, i.e. raised. Many such raised bogs can be seen in our flat valleys. They stand out as straw-coloured areas of wild vegetation contrasting with the surrounding bright-green of drained fields. A very good panorama with two large bogs can be seen from any high point above the valley from Mosedale to Mungrisdale, where Bowscale Moss and White Moss lie just outside the entrance of the River Caldew.

Curiosity took me to Cliburn Moss to see what I could find. A recently-dredged ditch showed a section through its history, and the clue to so much of it being exceedingly wet. At the base of the section was grey silty clay without any stones or bits in it: not boulder clay therefore but a clay that accumulated here in a shallow lake or river backwater as the Ice Age was dying. Then this became browner and peatier upwards, representing plant matter growing and dying in the water until the top part is pure peat. There was no real soil.

Cliburn Moss has old peat cuttings with square depressions, in which grow damp-loving sedges and reeds. On the banks are pine trees and on their dead stumps grow heathland plants. In the trees flocks of coal tits, blue tits and goldcrests twittered, despite the dark and rainy afternoon, and pine cones on the ground had been stripped by squirrels. I met recent deer tracks and a badger track.

Outside the trees is a dry area with heather and lichens, grading into damp moor and then into marsh and open water. Cranberry stems run riot over moss tussocks, and the edge of the marsh was pink with ragged robin having a late second flowering. At the point where cold wet water started trickling over the tops of my boots, indicating that I was about to get wetter than I had intended, there was masses of marsh cinquefoil, pennywort and valerian, though long past their flowering season. It is a place to revisit next summer.

16th November

Some plants and animals are known to me only from their illustrations in books. Creatures such as the Camberwell beauty butterfly, the dormouse, and the mink. I hope that when I do come across one of these, I'll recognise it straight away. Another species on this list was a fungus, the small orange stinkhorn going by the name of *Mutinus*, cousin to the well-known species but without the stink by which that one reveals its presence.

For very many years I have kept an eye open for it, but without ever having any success. Then this week, out of the blue - or rather out of a damp day in Melkinthorpe Wood - there it was.

I had entered the wood after a wet morning's walk, seeing flocks of fieldfares enjoying the berried bushes and scores of chaffinches feeding on the ground in the old lanes. Woodland was attractive in providing a bit of shelter from the rain, and from the choice of paths through the wood I chose the one through coniferous trees. This promised a dry picnic spot. However, having stopped for lunch, I ran out of motivation to continue. There seemed little of interest around and I decided to turn back.

Before doing so I had a quick look at the ground and fallen wood, and noticed some picturesque 'fairy' toadstools on a moss-covered tree stump. There was too little light really for photography, but with the help of a chunky piece of tree as an instant tripod it was worth trying. I turned my attention to the composition through the viewfinder and for the first time saw what appeared to be a very small stinkhorn 'egg' on the same stump.

Maybe, I thought, it's just a poorly-grown one. Perhaps it's been too dry to develop properly, perched up here. It didn't occur to me immediately that it might be something different. So I tried to confirm my defective conclusion by looking around for remains of the fungus. It was then that my eyes started to focus on several fully-grown, perfect specimens of *Mutinus caninus*, the little fungus whose picture I'd had in my head for so many years. And I had so very nearly turned round for home within sight of it.

23nd November

Monday this week deserves to go down in history as the day of the spider's web; the day when road signs and gates and hedges were decorated with white webs and looping strands like tinsel on a Christmas tree. I stopped in my tracks as I saw the wing mirrors of my car. Each had two white webs, heavy with frozen fog droplets. Each web was anchored at four corners with several strands of silk twisted into the main supporting lines. The resulting rectangular frames were infilled with triangles and kite-shaped spaces reminiscent of the 'cat's cradles' we used to make in a loop of string.

On Sunday night there had been up to 11 degrees of frost, and on Monday freezing fog coated the landscape with thick white frosting. Large birds were on the lookout for food, staking out likely places including gardens, car parks and roadsides. Black crows, rooks and jackdaws were easy to spot against the frost on roofs and fields, whereas flocks of seagulls blended in to the white world as they circled in the air.

A group of birds in the middle of a quiet road was gathered around a crow, which was eating what looked like a chunk of cake held firmly under its right foot. Each side of the crow stood a rook, watching and occasionally moving nearer the food but each time returning to their two-foot distance. This pair of rooks - could they be a true pair? - spent most time keeping a mob of jackdaws and seagulls at a distance, presumably so that if the crow should make a mistake the rooks would get first chance at the food. The jackdaws played the game of creeping in gradually, but were lunged at by the rooks and got nowhere. The seagulls tried sudden hit and run, flying straight through the mob to the crow's foot clutching the food. They had no success.

A group of jackdaws sitting peacefully on a fence let me walk right up to them. Would they take bread from my hand? I held out a piece and looked into the pale blue eyes of the nearest bird. He didn't move. I stretched my arm out a bit further towards him. I felt, before my eyes registered anything, a sharp slap on my fingers. The pale blue eyes in front of me never flickered as I withdrew my empty hand. My memory held the impression of a flurry of white wings over my hand, wings which I now saw receding into the distance and blending into the white of the landscape.

30th November

The beech tree at my side had a smooth grey-green trunk, ascending for twenty feet or so without a branch, and then continuing upwards and outwards to a great canopy. Now the leaves had fallen there was no shelter from the rain, and looking up into the tree from the ground was to look into a never-ending silver stream of raindrops.

A better position was enjoyed by the squirrel I was watching. It was sitting a long way above my head on a small ridge on the tree trunk, looking down at me as it chewed a nut. Its fluffy tail covered its back and head in the characteristic pose which is said to be the Greek origin of the name squirrel: skia-oura, or shadow-tail.

Despite the rain which was now turning to snow, there was plenty of bird activity in the woodland along the River Lowther. Groups of long-tailed tits with coal tits and blue tits noisily twittered their way from tree to tree, and treecreepers climbed silently upwards. A flash of white from the river bank caught my attention and I moved towards it. Two deer came towards me from a track down to the water, saw me, and trotted away. The sand at the water's edge bore their pointed footprints.

Looking at the tide-line of flood debris, the fresh heaps of plant stems on the banks or caught up in low tree branches, I estimated the river to have been 12 feet higher recently. The vegetation under that line looked battered and washed of all debris: fruits, seeds and bulbs included. How easy it must be, I thought, for waterside plants to spread downstream and colonise the places where their seeds eventually get washed up, and how difficult to spread the other way, upstream.

It was now snowing hard, and on leaving the wood for open fields I met the force of the wind and a complete white carpet over the ground. The snow stuck to my boots, wet and beginning to emit a creaking sound when walked on. How different this snow was from the old snow lying on the fells, which crunched underfoot, or the swish of the dry powder kind.

8th December

I have treated myself to a large coffee-table book: Richard Mabey's Flora Britannica. This is an account of all the flowers and trees in Britain, their everyday names, associations, uses and legends, as discovered from correspondants over five years of preparation. Its 400 pages are illustrated with colour photographs so good that I feel like giving up my own efforts at taking pictures. But they are not just artistic: they are a good guide to the identification of many wild flowers.

Common names have been enthusiastically collected. Many I knew, but I chuckled at 'devil's guts' for ground elder. My experience of digging up this weed is of no satisfaction at all: the roots don't follow any respectable pattern but are higgledy-piggledy, can't be pulled up as a clump like nettles nor as runners in the manner of convolvulus or couch-grass. Devilish indeed.

And the book reveals that 'forget-me-not' is not an old country name but a nineteenth-century invention for the plant previously called scorpion-grass.

Surprisingly, some trees and shrubs that have been with us from our prehistory to the present do not seem to have collected many names. Hornbeam is 'hardbeam', from the hardness of its wood and hazel the familiar 'lambs-tails'. Hazel nuts however give us the expression 'in a nutshell'. As Mabey expresses it, the nuts are an emblem of concentrated wisdom, something sweet, compact and sustaining enclosed in a small hard shell.

At the moment both these species stand out in our hedges and woodland margins, but for different reasons. The hornbeam is difficult to distinguish from beech when in leaf, but the fruits which are still falling, and can be seen amongst the fallen leaves on the ground, are unmistakeable. They are papery bunches of three-lobed scales, green becoming brown, with the seeds at the base of the scale. Hazel on the other hand is now covered in young catkins, as if ready to jump into action at the first breath of spring.

Each time I go out I see large flocks of fieldfares on the hawthorns and crab-apples, each still bearing masses of fruit. One hedgerow apple tree was occupied by around fifty chaffinches, eating from apples on the branches and on the ground. The yellow wrinkled apples were considerably larger than the cherry-like wild ones or the usual crabs. On tasting I found them as sweet as a cultivated variety, a discovery which the opportunist chaffinches were now so clearly enjoying.

14th December

It may sound strange, but I've found that looking down at the ground when walking under trees or by woodland margins often tells me what the trees are more than looking straight at them, and this is particularly true at this time of year. It doesn't take a genius to deduce that if there are oak leaves on the ground there must be an oak tree nearby. Similarly, dry cherry stones or empty half cherry shells point to the presence of cherry trees, and a look around can then pick out their trunks by the silverish colour and horizontal rings.

Last weekend I walked at the side of Whinfell Forest, and where large pine trees overlooked grassy fields the ground had big white splashes. There were also pellets containing rabbit remains, all suggesting that big birds, maybe the buzzards which were circling round high in the air, perch on this group of trees. Not looking ahead when walking is hazardous, and I got a shock when a hare dashed past my feet.

The landscape is so varied in Eden that a couple of hours took me from forest to moorland to lowland valley. After the depressing sight of very little water in our rivers through the summer, the deep, clear water now tumbling down makes them agreeable places for winter walking. For the last few weeks I have been exploring a stream to the south and east of Penrith. To be quite truthful, I hadn't realised that it was one and the same river at Cliburn, Melkinthorpe Wood and Little Strickland: the River Leith. It starts on the south side of the high ground at Shap and at first runs northward just like the River Lowther, but then bends east at Melkinthorpe and slips down into the low-lying ground by Cliburn Moss and into the Lyvennet.

Unlike on the River Eden, there were few ducks or geese to be seen, but I was delighted to see dippers, the little white-breasted birds which fly low over the water and land on a rock, bobbing up and down. What did resemble the Eden however was the extent of flat land alongside the river before the ground rises abruptly in the slope of a former bank at the edge of the valley. Across the River Eden from Lady's Walk at Edenhall is an great flat shelf between the river and this rise of the valley side, much frequented by geese, lapwings and oyster-catchers. I've been seeing similar flat fields along the Eamont and now particularly pronounced flats along the River Leith. At Cliburn this oddity can be seen from the road with the village perched on top of an ancient river bank of an impressive valley. The steep ancient bank can clearly be seen along the valley in both directions.

21st December

On a brilliantly sunny afternoon this week I deserted my desk to wander down to the trees and fields bordering the River Eamont near Stainton Island. I descended the steep path to the river through an open wood, where my attention was caught by a recently-broken ash tree, the break leaving a strip of strikingly white and clean wood. The annual growth rings were wide and clear, and I counted 35. A youngster, apparently healthy.

I looked around the debris of fallen trees. Many were equally young when they came down, but there were a few old, large trunks. I looked under the bark of one to confirm what had finished it off, and besides the black beetles and various tiny toadstools were the black 'bootlaces' I'd expected. These branched strands, looking like tough black sewing cotton, lie on the smooth surface of the wood, under the bark. They belong to the body of the honey fungus, which invades trees from an existing infected source and sends nutrients to feed the distant growing point, until it has got established in the new victim.

The sun was about to set, and the dried reeds along the river were picking up the gold light and looking most photogenic, so I moved on along the riverside fields. I noticed that the walls here were made of grey limestone, in contrast to the massive red sandstone cliff above the trees. I just made it in time to photograph some ducks as foreground to the sunset-lit water and shrubs, reminding me of the several occasions when I myself have paddled across to the island. It's a good place for wild flowers, weasels, moorhen families and spotted flycatchers. But now the sheeps' breath was forming white clouds, and it was too cold to loiter.

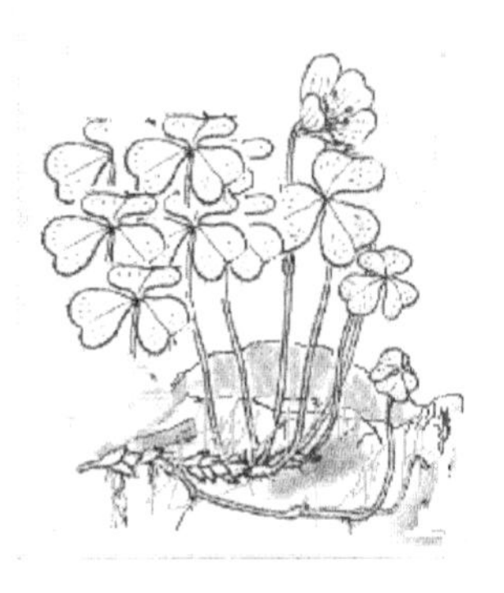

Behind me in the field a line of mole-hills stretched from the far boundary towards the river. The line appeared straight from a distance but close to could be seen to be making a slight curve. Do moles have a sense of direction underground? Towards the river were more mole hills, but this set made a cluster. I've rarely seen moles on the surface, and I started wondering if the two residents of this field met above ground.

It was time to do something about my total ignorance, so back to the bookshelf. There I read that moles can swim, and don't hibernate even at high altitudes, keeping on eating all winter. But I also learned that straight lines of mole-hills are made by males, and the groups by females. So maybe the two riverside neighbours will seek each other out next spring, if not sooner.

28th December

Christmas card scenes of white, green and red tints presented themselves in every direction. Snow on the hill-tops, frosted grass, icicles hanging from stream banks and plump robins looking out from the lower branches of holly trees still laden with berries. In the shadow of the valley bottom though the sun never rose, even at midday, and the beck was beginning to freeze. The ascent from Greenburn Bottom to Gibson Knott just along from the 'lion and lamb' above Grasmere was hard. The wind was icy, the ground iron-hard underfoot and my rucksac was weighed down with cameras as well as the heavy stainless-steel flask of coffee. All around however the hills were sunlit, and the stream and pools below in Greenburn Bottom were coloured apricot by the reflections of sunlit bracken.

Once over the top I was able to share the hot sunshine, and a short way down stopped at a giant boulder to take some pictures. Under the rock was a little garden of woodland plants: wood sorrel, fumitory, violets and ferns. In summer this would be a damp and shaded spot, but the very low midwinter sun went straight under the gap. Indeed, the ground there had thawed to decidedly soggy and a temporary rivulet ran from a boggy patch toward the valley.

Almost under my feet - which were on the driest patch around - there was a small yellow flower, apparently growing out of a cushion of moss. Of course it wasn't really, but its leaves had withered away and just three petals and three straw-coloured sepals sat on a tiny stalk. Inside the flower was a great pile of stamens with pollen. I wasn't as puzzled as I might have been, for the strangest thing was that the previous day I had lunched on a stream bank between Askham Common and Ullswater, and on the half-frozen bank by a waterfall was ... a little yellow flower.

That one had six petals, three stamens, and plenty of leaves and creeping stems. Although the flower measured only one centimetre across, and was a bit confused about its number of petals, it had all the distinguishing features of an ordinary creeping buttercup. And that's what this flower in Far Easedale was too. According to the floras, it does grow high up in mountains, but I found no reference to flowering in midwinter. There must be a lot more flowering as well as the ones I happened upon, and I'd be interested to hear from any reader who has more information. Meanwhile, it goes down on the list of things to be kept in mind next year.